Exploding the Reading

Building a world of responses from one small story,
50 interactive strategies for increasing comprehension

David Booth

Pembroke Publishers Limited

I thank the following friends for their technical and research support: Eleanor Gower, Bryan Wright, Sarah Papoff, and Jessica Lundy.

© 2014 Pembroke Publishers
538 Hood Road
Markham, Ontario, Canada L3R 3K9
www.pembrokepublishers.com

Distributed in the U.S. by Stenhouse Publishers
480 Congress Street
Portland, ME 04101
www.stenhouse.com

We acknowledge the financial support of the Government of Canada through the Canada Book Fund (CBF) for our publishing activities.

We acknowledge the assistance of the Government of Ontario through the Ontario Media Development Corporation's Ontario Book Initiative.

Library and Archives Canada Cataloguing in Publication

Booth, David W. (David Wallace), author
    Exploding the reading : building a world of strategies from one small story, 50 interactive strategies for increasing comprehension / David Booth.

Includes bibliographical references and index.
Issued in print and electronic formats.
ISBN 978-1-55138-299-9 (pbk.).--ISBN 978-1-55138-903-5 (pdf)

    1. Reading. 2. Comprehension. 3. Language arts. I. Title.

LB1050.B662 2014   428.4   C2014-903628-0
                                         C2014-903629-9

Editor: Kate Revington
Cover Design: John Zehethofer
Typesetting: Jay Tee Graphics Ltd.

Printed and bound in Canada
9 8 7 6 5 4 3 2 1

MIX
Paper from
responsible sources
FSC® C004071

Contents

THE SEALPELT, OR SELSHAMURINN:

A Version of the Selchie Tale from Iceland

In the Icelandic myths, seals are believed to be condemned by humans. One ancient story from the south of Iceland is about a farmer who early one morning finds a sealpelt lying on the beach. In a cave nearby, he hears voices and music. He takes the sealpelt home and hides it in a wooden chest. A few days later he returns to the beach and finds a crying, naked, young woman sitting on a rock. He brings her to his house, where she stays, but he never tells her about the pelt. As time goes by, they get married and have children. But the young woman is restless and often stares quietly out of the window at the ocean. One day when the farmer goes fishing, his wife accidentally finds the key of the chest, opens it, and discovers the missing pelt. She takes leave of her children, puts the pelt on, and before she dives into the ocean, she says: "I am very anxious, with seven children on land and seven in the sea." She never comes back, but the farmer misses her terribly. Later when he goes fishing, there often is a seal near his boat, and its eyes are filled with tears. It is said that the farmer becomes a very lucky fisherman. And when his children play at the beach, there often is a seal swimming close to land. Sometimes, it brings them beautiful stones and colorful fishes. But their mother never returned.

Ása Helga Ragnarsdóttir
Assistant lecturer in drama and theatre education
University of Iceland, School of Education

INTRODUCTION

How One Story Can Generate a Thousand Responses

What can we learn from having 40 teachers and 1000 students exploring one text at the same time in different school districts in Ontario, New Brunswick, and the Northwest Territories? This book examines *responding to text* in these K to 12 classrooms in order to observe how different teachers can work with a particular text selection to enable their students to respond individually, in groups, or as part of a shared whole-class event.

We know that every reader interacts with a text by making a personal and individual response, but as a teacher-researcher, I am interested in how those responses alter, extend, grow, and expand when we incorporate different modes of interacting with the text, especially with others who have read, listened to, or viewed it, as well. Choice of response modes will vary depending upon the text, student needs, student interests, the context for the experience, and the teacher's comfort zone and experience with different forms, formats, and media. I want to encourage teachers to incorporate a variety of response modes in their teaching of different types of texts.

In this book, Kindergarten through high-school students respond to the same story. This structure allows us to explore these questions:

- How will we as teachers help the students to work within the text, move outside the text, and then return to the text with deeper understanding?
- What will different groups take from each tale?
- What meanings will individual students take away from the experience?
- What will the artifacts of their experiences with the story — poems, oral tellings, visuals, blogs, art, transcripts, comparisons, research, conversations, or role-play — tell us so that we can extend our own repertoires of useful response modes for our students?

Entering Worlds of Meaning

In 2011, Tara-Lynn Scheffel, from Nipissing University, and I spent some time with a similar project, where we had a novel reprinted chapter by chapter in the community newspaper for students in the North Bay area to choose to read.

Exploding the Reading is built around a single universal story, told in several versions and formats, about selchies, mythic creatures of the northern seas, who once a year take human form; thus was created the Selchie Project. This folktale has been a staple of storytellers for years, and its minimal narrative leaves much to explore through a variety of response modes.

What interests me is how children take from a story or a film only what they can process themselves. *The Lion King* is a good popular example: on stage, the puppets are the best I have ever seen, and they thrill the children and adults. Few kids are worried about the evils of colonization as they watch, but some older ones are, and the adults' responses vary according to their life experiences.

Making Meaning with Texts: Selected Essays represents the theory of Louise Rosenblatt, who has had an enormous influence on how we engage our students in negotiating meaning making with the texts they encounter. Response theory grows from her seminal studies on comprehension as an interactive process.

The insights emerging from the Selchie Project grow from the variety and range of students' responses as we look at the differences in the ages and stages of childhood, and yet find surprising commonalities. As a reader of *Exploding the Reading*, you will find that one text can, indeed, generate a thousand responses from students who have encountered it, depending on the context of the interaction. I have included different teaching/learning experiences with this folktale, discovering alongside the classes the learning that happens when we go beyond the words into worlds of meaning that develop and accrue from "diving into the deep end of the pool."

Looking Back to See Ahead

I began by rereading my own thoughts on response to text, found over the years in my own writings, but never had I focused entirely on this aspect of literacy growth. A few years ago, my colleague Bob Barton and I wrote *Story Matters*, in which we developed our framework for a response repertoire. We organized the types of activities with which children could be engaged into 10 categories, or modes, of communication. These are reflected in the structure of this book. Here, I have collected bits and pieces from my previous writings on response to text and used them as anchors for adding my changing and deepening understanding of how response to text can function in contemporary classrooms.

I owe Ellin Oliver Keene a great debt because of her book *To Understand: New Horizons in Reading Comprehension*. She writes with elegance and eloquence in her conversations about literacy, weaving in her own life experiences that demonstrate the strong values of a literary and literacy education.

As I selected those past pieces of commentary and reflection on responding to texts, I realized how far we have come in discussing the value of student voice and personal interpretation as agents for meaning making; I also saw how supportive our response activities can be in expanding a student's comprehension of a text. I felt this construct would work as a plan for exploring a single text in many different classrooms, with different grades. I was able to add to, rework, and extend my thoughts, enriched by my visiting or discussing with teachers and students in different grades in 30 classrooms, and observing their explorations growing from one story, represented in different versions, from oral tellings to picture books to complex ballads. The responses of the different students could be examined within the frame of the 10 different modes, and we would be able to notice the ages and stages of development as seen in the students' work.

Opening up voice through response modes

Gordon Wells, a colleague and friend for several years, had a strong influence on my work with response to texts, and his books *The Meaning Makers: Learning to Talk and Talking to Learn* and *Dialogic Inquiry: Towards a Socio-Cultural Practice and Theory of Education*, on my bookshelves forever, are still foundations for understanding how children make meaning.

In each telling of a story, the *story truth* will usually remain, but the voices will be unique to the specific experience. The heart of this project lies in the responses of the students: even though we all began with the same basic tale, each student has conjured up a slightly different story event determined by his or her past life and previous text experiences; at the same time, however, the societal truths of the tale can be found in the art of Kindergarten children (Laura Siwak's "The Inquiry Process in Kindergarten"), in the role-play of Grade 7 students (Grant Minkhorst's "How Creating Backstories Strengthens Students' Oral Reading"), and in the issues-driven debate of Grade 9 young people (Pina Marchese's "Interpreting Text through Argument and Debate"). As the students revealed and explored their personal interpretations with others, their personal stories may have altered, grown, become reframed, or extended. That is one of the joys of being together in the place we call school.

As teachers, we need to be aware of the range and of the merits and drawbacks of the choices we could give to or ask of students to expand their understandings of the text they have encountered. Traditionally, they have read and answered

How much can we learn from working inside the text, then moving outside the textual frame, and then returning to the text with new-found perceptions and insights and information? This focus has been my work over the last 40 years.

questions where answers may be found in the text, or they have become involved in activities that do not connect back to the original text. For example, book reports occur after finishing a book, generally during independent reading, often done at home — but I seldom see evidence of how students have expanded on the ideas generated by their first reading of the text. On the other hand, literature circles and book clubs, in person or online, offer opportunities to hear other viewpoints and to rethink one's original position on the ideas in the text with small groups of readers. Shared reading and discussion as a class can do the same, and moving into research on the Internet and exploring the deep issues and relationships in the text can move the students a long way forward in their understanding and meaning making. I wanted to become involved in sharing a text with students in order to expand their collective and personal meaning-making, their continually developing understanding of what they have experienced.

The first reading of a text is not "a done deal" — students can have so many different interpretations of their original reading experience. How exciting and involving it can be when they begin to explore the impact of that text on their meaning-making lives!

The Folktale as Text

I have chosen one folktale as the text: it is readily available online and in print, with lots of versions, different genres, different modes, with so many issues to catch our attention. A tale can be the beginning for exploring all the ways we as educators have for encouraging students to dig deeply inside the story and to discover the surrounds outside that particular text — the origins, the connections, the places, the values, the different perceptions readers have, the language structures — and to transpose that original text into other forms that let us look as if with different and critical eyes, to ponder what might have been, to challenge the information, to add the new learning to our construct of the world. I like the phrase "It takes two to read a book." We may need to bounce ideas off others to find out our deeper thoughts and to rethink our views.

Storyteller Bob Barton says that these "stories of the tribe" provide strong reading and listening materials for children. The context of long ago enables children to explore a variety of problems and concerns that have troubled humanity forever, but in a safe, non-threatening framework. The deeds of heroes, the schemes of tricksters, the lore of nations past . . . these can all serve as settings for the children's own development — family situations, societal difficulties, supernatural beliefs, and natural phenomena. Folktales or contemporary stories with folk quality help the children journey to another time: an imagined past, an analogous present, or an anticipated future. The words can offer powerful language learning for the child, story vocabulary, new and varied syntactic patterns, strong contextual clues (which permit them to explore meaning), and characters who struggle with life's problems, sometimes symbolic, sometimes very real. With such stories, the children are engaged in experiencing language more complex than their own.

Folktales have acquired significance as they passed through time. Stories of today are built on stories of the past. Folktales allow us to use their "bones" as they speak to the child in all of us, symbolizing deep feelings and using fantastic figures and events. No matter how ancient a story is, it's not just archeological remains (see Chapter 12), but a living tale we can examine, offering glimpses of a particular time or a particular culture.

Ása Helga Ragnarsdóttir is assistant lecturer in drama and theatre education, University of Iceland, School of Education. According to her, the story of the selchie people dates back to 1862 when Jón Árnason, the Icelandic folklore collector, published *Icelandic Folklore and Fairy Tales*. Árnason collected stories all over the country: stories that had been told man by man over the decades and of which no one knew the author. The stories attracted much attention and greatly influenced the nation's image and the independence efforts of Icelanders over the next hundred years.

Yolen, Jane. 1981. *Touch Magic: Fantasy, Faerie and Folklore in the Literature of Childhood*. New York: Philomel Books.

A living tale open to multiple responses

I want to involve the students in response modes that suit them, their progress, and wherever possible, their interests. For this project, some teachers had students researching aspects underlying the story; other students worked on interpreting and representing through visual arts or role-play; still others explored how to retell the tale in various ways: orally, in film, or through written forms. What will be helpful to you as a reader of this book is the range of responses, the variety of modes that encourage expression, rethinking, analyzing, and reflecting. Whether the experience lasts a period, a succession of periods, a day, or a week, we can gain so much from the students' thoughts and feelings and articulations about their reactions and responses to one story.

I found many versions of the selchie tale (some listed in the Appendix). These include tellings by Jane Yolen, Mordicai Gerstein, and Susan Cooper, which may be in your school library. There are also many versions to be found on the Internet, some ballads captured in song, and other stories connected by theme. As with all folktales and picture-book versions, the story addresses both child and adult. Sometimes the selchie is a woman; other times a young boy, and in one of the ballads, the husband of a human wife. But all the stories center on the interactions and the relationships between humans and sea people, the strangers who come to our shores.

And what is a story? Something with a beginning, a middle and an end, of course. But the lasting stories are more. If they are lacking that bit of "inner truth," then they are of no value. Without meaning, without metaphor, without reaching out to touch human emotion, a story is a poor thing: a few rags upon a stick masquerading as a living creature. Storytelling is our oldest form of remembering the promises we have made to one another and to our various gods, and the promises given in return; it is a way of recording our human emotions and desires and taboos. Whoever dares to tell a story must bear in mind that the story is an essential part of our humanness. But of course it had better be an engrossing, well-told tale as well.

Jane Yolen, in *Touch Magic*, p. 25

Which Modes for Which Class?

In Chapters 3 through 12, you will meet teachers who have explored this tale with their classes, sometimes as a single lesson, other times as a longer unit. The teachers chose the modes of response that fit their curriculum expectations, or drew on the interests of the students, or introduced their students to a new or different way of thinking about this text. As some say in their articles, this is work-in-progress, within the frame of regular classroom work, sometimes with polished results, other times as organic processing. All of the responses can help us, regardless of the grades we teach, to observe the ideas and articulations of students, their stages of development, their values and beliefs, and their abilities with language and with artistic ways of communicating. And perhaps, their explorations will offer us new ways of approaching texts, different options for encouraging thoughtful responses, and a strengthening of our professional mandate for supporting and encouraging deep, skillful representations of learning.

Varied teacher approaches

How each teacher shared the story was important. Did they read some of the tale and discuss it with the students? Did they read right through and then begin student responses? Did they prepare the students with some background for setting up the story experience? Did they show a YouTube clip on the great seals? Did they simply tell the story, children on a rug, the teacher wrapped in a cloth that represented the seal skin? The units they developed focused on fish, on fishermen, on the seas, on seals, and on transformations. We want to see responses that grow from their units or story, and to consider the depths young students can plumb.

Each teacher had the students respond to the story using a variety of different modes. The students responded as a class, in a group, or independently. Teachers either wrote up the experience with student work, or I wrote it up from our discussions.

How students have responded

I have sought to represent students from regular classrooms responding to text, deepening their comprehension, extending their meaning making, offering and changing opinions, making connections, researching data, using graphics, telling and retelling, reading aloud, writing in different genres, incorporating visual arts and music, role-playing, summarizing, analyzing — all the processes that we understand will support our students as thoughtful, critical readers and writers, who share informed opinions, who represent their ideas and feelings in aesthetic and artistic ways, and who recognize the power of words used well.

Best practices for implementing response modes

In my last few books, I have been fortunate to write alongside wonderful teachers, and here, I am continuing this approach from my position as participant, onlooker, and writer. There are 10 modes for responding. In Chapters 3 through 12, we will briefly discuss how to use each mode in a classroom. You will then find accounts of effective classroom lessons and units with students' voices represented in a transcript, through the arts, or as written work. This format can encourage all of us to continue our work as meaning makers with all types of genres and forms of text, and a great variety of responses.

This book, then, includes best practice examples of literacy learning and teaching, all drawn from a tale 200 years old, supported by a variety of connected texts, and most important, by responses from a thousand students. I am hoping that, as you read different accounts of colleagues, you will continue to expand your own repertoire of modes for student involvement with different texts. The ideas and suggestions grow from real classroom experiences generated by authentic expertise. But first, let us consider the meaning-making power of student response and its relationship to comprehension (Chapter 1) and aspects of organizing a response-based classroom (Chapter 2).

CHAPTER 1

The Meaning-Making Power of Student Response

We are redefining our concepts about literacy, not just in schools but in all the contexts of our lives. We interpret and construct all kinds of *texts* to express our ideas, information, instructions, feelings, and opinions: books, documents, conversations, orders, speeches, instructions, photos, graphics, television, blogs, music, and radio.

Then we use different *modes* to communicate our ideas: spoken words, written words, images, sounds, and multimodes, or combinations of modes (e.g., videos, Facebook, ads, movies, and games).

We want students to discover the options these can bring to their worlds of communication. Even our definition of *book* has changed: electronic readers, including phones, are popular ways of reading print texts now, as well as "reading" images and sounds.

As a result, we will have to adapt our strategies for supporting students as interactive "readers" who can respond to these new modes, from blogs to wikis to technological art forms. This need to adapt our ways of supporting students applies to their constructing and composing processes, as well. E-writing is ubiquitous, something I can testify to as I write this book on a laptop with a spell check and Internet resources at hand.

Dynamic Interactions with Text

As they interact with each text, readers bring their unique personal backgrounds and concerns. In a sense, they make the text fit their meaning-making strategies or cognitive frameworks for organizing and interpreting data. The teacher's role is to empower students to wander inside and around the selection, to wonder about it, to make meaningful connections, to question it, to deepen their understanding of it, to explore its ideas, its content, its forms and formats. Students need to explore the text and try to relate what they have experienced to their own lives, accepting, challenging, noting, confirming, wondering, feeling moved or surprised. They negotiate their own meaning-making connections.

Communication has always meant more than just words. Visual images — the view of the street, the picture in the advertisement, the action on the screen — often convey the larger part of the message. Parents, teachers, and book publishers have long recognized that pictures are important for young children, but only recently has exploration of "the media" — television, film, magazines, and especially the technology screen — been seen as an integral part of the learning continuum.

In terms of literacy teaching, our students are not learning to be literate the way we did or the generation before us did. Today's students are familiar with a much broader range of texts, both print and electronic, than we ever were. In their world, the written word has been extended by the visual, the aural, and the tactile. We need only to think about different readers' responses to a newspaper article, a YouTube video, a political speech, a new CD, a religious film, or a novel, to realize that each text requires interpretation if meanings are to be made. The reader's encounter with a text is a dynamic interaction, depending on many factors.

What effective literacy practices enable

Luke, Allan, and Peter Freebody. 1999. "A Map of Possible Practices." *Practically Primary* 4, 5–8.

According to Allan Luke and Peter Freebody, effective literacy draws on a repertoire of practices that allow learners, as they engage in reading and writing activities, to do the following:

- *to break the code of texts:* recognizing and using the fundamental features and architecture of written texts, including alphabet, sounds in words, spelling, conventions, and patterns of sentence structure and text;
- *to participate in the meanings of text:* understanding and composing meaningful written, visual, and spoken texts from within the meaning systems of particular cultures, institutions, families, communities, nation-states, and so forth;
- *to use texts functionally:* traversing the social relations around texts; knowing about and acting on the different cultural and social functions that various texts perform both inside and outside school and knowing that these functions shape the way texts are structured, their tone, their degree of formality, and their sequence of components;
- *to critically analyze and transform texts:* understanding and acting on the knowledge that texts are not neutral, that they represent particular views and silence other points of view, influence people's ideas; and that their designs and discourses can be critiqued and redesigned, in novel and hybrid ways.

The linguistic and cultural differences that different texts present offer us a wealth of opportunities, an enrichment of possibilities. As we recognize the complexities of society's issues, we see the need for "reading" at the deepest level, for recognizing the shades of grey between black-and-white extremes. Those who read only minimal text in any form or format are susceptible to control by corporations, unethical political leaders, or charlatans. Literacy is a foundation of citizenry in any language — a right of freedom. An informed citizenry requires competency in many different text forms.

In the following article, student work-study teacher Elaine Vodarek describes how students of various ages interact with texts in dynamic ways made possible by technology.

APP POWER: RESPONDING TO TEXTS IN MULTIMODAL WAYS

Elaine Vodarek

Having an iPad in the classroom has transformed the way students are able to respond to text. Traditionally, when assessing students' responses to various texts, students were required to write responses, or when opportunities were available to listen to the texts and record anecdotal notes, they could respond orally. Now, using the Explain Everything app on the iPad, students are able to interact with text in more dynamic ways. Students who could understand big ideas, identify key themes, make rich connections, and ask relevant questions to further understanding during discussion, but who often struggled to communicate their understanding well in writing have benefited from being able to record their thinking in alternative ways.

The Explain Everything app is capable of recording audio, video, typed text, and written text, as well as photos, all on one page. Because it can capture written and oral communication and be saved in a variety of ways, it has been a great resource to use when documenting and reflecting on student thinking and learning. Student responses can also be shared with groups or a whole class, using a *dongle* (a connection cable between the iPad and projector), and feedback can be given immediately.

HOW VARIOUS CLASSES USE THE EXPLAIN EVERYTHING APP

Since I was working as a student work study teacher in a variety of classrooms, I will provide a brief overview of a few ways students have been using the Explain Everything app.

In a Grade 1 class, students were often asked to write or draw in response to a prompt or question based on a shared text, usually a picture book. Rylan, for one, often struggled to get his ideas down on paper, but conversationally, he demonstrated an understanding of what he was meant to do. By recording the prompt, in both audio and typed forms, Rylan was able to listen to the prompt over again as needed. If an illustration in the shared book was helpful to respond to the prompt, he could take the camera tool in Explain Everything and insert the photo as part of his response. He was able to draw arrows between the parts of the prompt and the parts of the corresponding picture, and explain his thinking orally, using the audio-record feature.

In a Grade 4/5 class, the Explain Everything app was used to capture students' thinking about critical questions related to an embedded video. The Playing For Change website was embedded into a page in the app, and students were able to watch the music videos (*Stand By Me* and *Imagine*) and explore what the organization, which promotes peace through music, does. They could use the screen capture tool to take photos of information they found interesting or considered important. When responding to critical questions about the music videos, the organization, and social justice, students were able to use the various tools in Explain Everything to capture their thinking: they used a combination of still photos, written annotations, and oral recordings. Many students preferred being able to express themselves using multimedia in this way.

Grade 8 students also benefited from using the app during their language sessions. In this particular class, some students had their own iPads, while others were able to sign them out from the library (10 were available through the library). The Grade 8 students would use the camera tool to take a photo of the text they were responding to and then make annotations on the text using the pen tool. They could record their thinking in point form and highlight specific information they planned to use in their responses. Taking it further, students would then search out additional information to validate and support their thinking and provide links to their evidence. Final responses to the text could be written or appear in a more graphic form that included quotes, personal thoughts, and links to support and images. Students' work could be shared with the whole class, using a projector, and the topic could be explored further, using the students' work as a conversation starter.

Allowing students in Grades 1 through 8 to respond to text in alternative ways has improved students' engagement and the quality and depth of their thinking. Students felt they were able to capture more using a variety of tools, all housed in one app, than if they were only writing responses to texts. Being able to share their work, see others' work, and talk about their responses gave them an audience other than just the teacher and allowed them to refine their thinking and express themselves more comprehensively in subsequent tasks. Having a record of their thinking within the Explain Everything app meant that there was evidence of student thinking that could be reflected on and referred to at a later date, if need be, too.

Exploding Comprehension

Serafini, Frank, and Suzette Youngs. 2008. *More (Advanced) Lessons in Comprehension*. Portsmouth, NH: Heinemann.

In *More (Advanced) Lessons in Comprehension*, Frank Serafini and Suzette Youngs write: "Comprehending is a process of actively constructing meaning in transaction with texts in a particular social context. These processes begin with the noticing or perception of textual and visual elements and end with the construction and reconsideration of meanings" (p. 1).

We seldom read the same text twice in the same way: we bring our new experiences to each interpretation of the text, negotiating and constructing our ideas as we interact with others, with our own puzzlements, and with our efforts to assimilate our developing responses with our own backgrounds. Effective readers strive to bring different perspectives to their meaning making with a text, recognizing the interplay of personal connections, text connections, and world connections in their comprehending processes. The deeper the text, the more complex these processes become, and the learning of what it means to be a proficient reader can grow exponentially.

We want to introduce students to a variety of texts and modes that will support their ever-expanding understanding of the particular text they are encountering. In so doing, we provide them with opportunities to deepen their comprehension, to change, add to, appreciate, modify, enrich, or confront their initial responses through the rethinking and reworking processes involved in constructing their thoughts within a particular response mode. (Chapter 2 expands on the use of comprehension strategies inside the response modes.)

Initiating and Supporting Deep Responses from Students

Our comprehension alters as our life goes on, and our response to a text is never frozen. The landscape of our minds is constantly shifting as we read, when we reflect on what we have read, when we explore our own interpretations through different modes, and when we consider the ideas and opinions of others. In the quest for promoting deep understanding, we don't just "teach" a particular text: we use it — a book, an article, a picture book, an audio speech, a film, a newspaper report, or a YouTube video — as a stimulus for exploring ideas and issues within the text and in our expanding perceptions as we move outside the frame of the text. Gordon Wells says: "As the learner appropriates the knowledge and procedures encountered in interaction with others, he or she transforms them, constructing his or her own personal version. But in the process, he or she is also transformed" (p. 127).

Wells, Gordon. 1994. *Changing Schools from Within*. Portsmouth, NH: Heinemann.

Years ago, reading expert Charles Reasoner taught us "to help readers reveal their comprehension." When students grow as readers and viewers of texts of all types and genres, they can reveal their thoughts, ideas, and feelings about a selection. When these literacy experiences are extended and supported through their own spoken, written, and artistic responses, students are moving into the field of interpretation, appreciation, and critical and creative thought, understanding the negotiation that is required in order to participate in reading what others have constructed. They are learning to consider the complexities involved in the relationship between text and reader.

Teachers can help their students explore their personal responses inside, outside, and all around the text. The opportunities students have for responding to a text mean that they can rethink and reconsider the text they have encountered. They may extend, deepen, modify, or change their own responses through conversations, book clubs, literature circles, blogs, dialogue journals, Internet research, interviews, art, drama, and so on. Students can bring new understanding to the text through exploring the ideas and structures, representing new thoughts, and transferring their developing meanings through another mode.

Through carefully designed response activities, we can move students into different, divergent, critical, and deeper levels of thinking, feeling, and learning. We can discover with our students what they think they saw and heard and felt, helping them come to grips with their own and others' perceptions, and rethink and rework their initial reactions. The printed or visual text, the conversation text, and the students' constructed response texts wrap us, as readers, in layers of new meanings.

As students work with a text, they add their voices to the meaning making, bringing their own life experiences in conversation with the ideas the text has generated. Through their talk, inquiries, graphic representations, written responses, artistic representations, role-playing, and connected readings, students find their language and their thinking respected and valued. They are active and involved agents in making sense of what they are experiencing and learning: the hallmark of effective readers. Through authentic responses, they can question the text, uncover biases, and connect issues to their own lives, cultures, and communities. By allowing and encouraging student responses, the voice of every reader or viewer can be represented on issues of social justice, gender, faith, and culture.

Forms of student response

What we look for in responses to reading are instances where students do any of the following:

- They gossip about, reflect on, and comment on the texts.
- They challenge previous notions they had about a topic.
- They gain new learning through interacting with others.
- They discover a new way of viewing a character or an event.
- They see the text in a larger, critical context.
- They check the accuracy of their predictions.
- They consider questions that were answered and others that were unanswered.
- They think about what they have gained from reading and link it to their existing knowledge.
- They question, compare, evaluate, and draw conclusions from their reading of the text.
- They represent their interpretations in a different mode, such as visual art, film, or poetry.

- They discuss their connections to the text — the events, the context, the impact.
- They talk about other modes that this text conjures up, as well as other genres, versions, themes, styles, authors, cultures, even text structures, such as novels written as free verse.
- They share presentations, seminars, and debates about the text issues.
- They discuss the authors and the ideas and people they have written about, and discover background information that supports the authors.
- They brainstorm, problem-solve, and make decisions about issues and problems depicted in the text.
- They explore feelings and thoughts both inside and outside the text.

Questions for Us as Teachers to Consider

- Do we encourage different ways of participating in print-focused contexts, modeling and demonstrating alternative possibilities for literacy behaviors? What else might we do?
- Are we becoming aware of the changes in students' literacy lives, in the texts, the formats, the forms, the genres, the interweaving of text forms, the newly invented vocabulary, the words that have become unfamiliar from lack of use, the group dynamics that promote or defeat our efforts, the popular texts, the enrichment texts we believe in, and students' heartfelt and mindful responses to the variety of texts they will encounter?
- Are we advocating for those readers in difficulty who would benefit from supportive technologies and programs?
- Are we extending our awareness of the changes in students' literacy lives through conducting action research in our classrooms, gaining professional development, and reading appropriate information in journals and in online resources?
- Are we each morphing into a literacy teacher that our students will remember with respect (and even affection), after they have moved on in their lives?

Strong Motivation to Learn

Students can learn to approach each text they meet both critically and creatively. As they seek opportunities for expressing their thoughts and feelings, what they think and how they respond should matter to them and to us. A sense of competence and a developing belief in their own abilities to learn will build their confidence and increase their motivation. Students learn to co-construct knowledge through membership in an evolving community, to persist and concentrate in accomplishing their work, and to take satisfaction from their achievements. Students may connect personally to the texts they encounter, drawing on their backgrounds and experiences, becoming agents of their own learning. They can express and explore their developing selves, with opportunities to discover ideas that can affect their lives. Furthermore, their literacy proficiency grows as they read, write, talk, paint, film, and construct, for authentic reasons, recognizing that strategies for making meaning with text forms are requisite in articulating positions and opinions, and in being understood. Students are recognizing their own roles and responsibilities as learners.

CHAPTER 2

Organizing a Response-Based Classroom

Teachers can incorporate learning strategies that will engage students in thoughtful dialogue and discussion as a class, in groups, and with partners, in projects that are shared through conferences or presentations in person or online, and in constructing responses in a variety of media alone and with others that move the students into both wider and deeper reading dispositions. These opportunities may challenge the students' personal thinking and that of their peers in meaningful ways, so that they are constantly reflecting on their learning, increasing, altering, modifying, and extending their understanding through collaborative and cooperative events.

Strengthening a Community of Literacy Partners

All students in a classroom must feel that they are part of the reading community. Even pre-readers can sense that they are somehow part of the print world — listening, joining in, and rehearsing the reading process with well-known stories that they select and hold and turn the pages of. For all students in each grade, belonging to the reading community, or literacy club, requires success with printed text at every age and stage of development, along with success in other text modes. They need all kinds of materials in their classrooms to gain access to the worlds of print, image, and sound, and these resources must connect to the satisfaction of making sense of texts. Students learn to read in the pursuit of genuine purposes.

We want our students to work towards independence, to develop into lifelong readers who see texts either online or in print as friendly objects, who recognize the art of reading, as Louise Rosenblatt, the authority on reader response, said, as the negotiation between the reader and the text. How can we help students think carefully about the texts they read, to become aware of how each text and each mode works?

Offer different kinds of reading experiences

We can set up conditions whereby the students are able to see themselves as readers of all kinds of text forms. We can provide times for these kinds of reading:

- regular private reading, when students select texts and read silently;
- group reading, when several students discuss the same text or a number of texts connected by author, theme, culture, or pattern;
- shared reading with genre- and theme-connected units, where the whole class participates; and
- audience reading, when text is shared aloud with a group or with the whole class.

Work with the whole class some of the time

We need to incorporate physical and timetable arrangements that benefit as many students as possible and as often as possible. As teachers, we participate in the literacy events of the classroom, sometimes reading to the whole class, or leading students in song, showing videos, and using the interactive whiteboard or projector to demonstrate and share strategies. But even during those collaborative events, we observe the students — their behaviors, their attitudes, and their individual focusing abilities — so that we can assess and organize future literacy events that will support them into further learning.

Effective teachers have always supported students with individual needs, abilities, and interests, but much is good about working with the whole class some of the time:

- Discuss the issues that arise from reading and research, the planning of the week's schedule, and the modeling of strategy use (e.g., how to question a text or explore differing perceptions).
- Introduce students to and have them explore whole-class units built around themes and genres that offer unique opportunities to observe the students in a large-group setting: their level of participation, their ability to follow a discussion, their ability to raise relevant issues, and their use of strategies for understanding. Beyond that, observe their participation in reading and writing workshops designed to expand on and deepen a unit.
- Present mini-lessons and demonstrations; plan for seminars with the teacher and students who are sharing information and ideas; and give book talks featuring new resources.
- Have students present their inquiries, personal writing, debates, and projects they have constructed to the whole class.
- Build drama lessons around significant themes and issues, and enable presentations by students who have important work to share.
- Arrange for films and for guests in the room and on Skype.

Reading and Responding in Groups

More than 40 years ago, noted educator James Moffett said we need to make the solitary acts of reading and writing *socially constructed events* if we want to promote literacy development in young people. The *peer group imperative* demonstrated every day by our students may be our greatest classroom asset.

There is such satisfaction in watching developing readers enter a discussion with a group about a shared selection. They begin to notice how they create meaning, to wrestle with ideas, to prove a point by reading a portion of the text, to ask questions about the comments of group members, to draw inferences from the discussion and the words on the page, and to gain insights from their own experiences with print. Students are constructing meaning together, making sense of their responses to what they have read and heard, mediated by the ideas and feelings of group members. Reading has become an interactive process, a socially constructed learning experience. All members of the class, including us as teachers, are part of the classroom community of readers and writers.

Response experiences in groups can be transformative in students' lives: the student builds on others' talk, takes turns, recognizes points of view, carries the conversation forward, modifies and adapts ideas, links to the ideas of others, explores and questions, accepts or adopts the role of group leader, initiates

In *Deeper Reading: Comprehending Challenging Texts, 4–12*, Kelly Gallagher presents strategies for rereading texts for deeper understanding, and for encouraging thoughtful response activities.

conversation with the teacher, looks for alternative solutions and suggests new lines of discussion, reveals feelings, shares personal anecdotes, and relates new information to known. This interplay among learners supports meaning making in every discipline and creates shared understandings as individuals recognize how their own views and perceptions affect the thinking of the other participants in the learning.

Affirm the importance of group work

There are ways to strengthen the group work. You can move about the room, questioning groups, challenging ideas, promoting deeper thought, communicating ideas between groups, resetting a problem, defining a focus. You may structure the task-centered problem-solving in pairs or in small groups, encouraging student-to-student interactions.

I have learned, though, it is important to call the groups back together to check on what has been happening. "What discussion has your group had?" "Did everyone agree?" "What caused your group to think this way?" "Do you agree with what the other groups have said?" The students must feel that what occurred during the group time is important to them personally and to the class as a whole.

The greatest growth in the students' understanding often occurs when the whole class is working together and where small-group work helps deepen the meaning making for that experience in the community.

Independent Reading and Responding

Today, schools include independent reading opportunities in a variety of ways, and students are benefiting from the time, resources, and support that enable this program to be successful. In independent reading, it is important that students be able to select texts that connect to their interests, so that they can move deeply into the narrative or the information, making interpretations of their own, classifying and categorizing the new data, identifying with characters, living their own lives inside the printed (or screen) pages, constructing their own opinions. Choice and voice are strongly connected.

Provide some structure

I prefer independent reading time to have some structure. Some students need more encouragement, and others may need assistance in choosing or reading more books or more difficult books, or finding texts they can handle easily.

We can guide the selection and increase students' reading proficiency through book talks, individual conferences, and mini-lessons, and through promoting reading journals, where we dialogue with students as co-readers of a special text.

Arrange for the sharing of independent reading

One way to strengthen the literacy community is to call the students together to share and support one another's independent reading. We can invite students to read aloud favorite parts of their books or to comment on the characters or the issues they are uncovering as they read. We often read alone, but our power as literate humans can be developed from the connections we make sharing in the responses and comments of other community members.

Writing a book report is often used as a testing device, but it can have value as a teaching strategy. After reading the text, the student might write a report as an outgrowth of the reading and conversations with other readers about that text or

Jeffrey Wilhelm has written several books with strategies for promoting significant and relevant responses in students, including *You Gotta Be the Book: Teaching Engaged and Reflective Reading with Adolescents.* He understands the need for using student interests as the basis for text exploration.

other texts being discussed, or as a piece based on thoughtful reflections drawn from the student's reading journal. Through the report, the student can consider the text in light of the experiences surrounding it — a far cry from announcing "I liked it" or "I didn't like it."

How rich responses can become when students move beyond a traditional book report and instead, make an authentic response to their reading! Students may be able to see their ideas in print accompanied by images, drawn or found online, watching what they thought they knew change and alter in the moment through the very act of responding! The qualities of the powerful texts they encounter — the words, the style, the issues, the alternative points of view — offer them added strength for constructing their own arguments and meaning-making compositions. Students begin to notice and perhaps appreciate the art of writing, where words crafted with care and compassion can create an aesthetic and intellectual response to issues of the human condition, and where images communicate complicated processes and feelings. The response can illuminate the learning begun with the reading of the text.

Offering Rich Resources for Rich Perspectives

Students need to encounter rich resources to develop their personal and global understandings, to increase their frames around important topics and issues. We can provide access to technology, books (both fiction and nonfiction), newspapers and magazines, the Internet, films and television, and guests (in person and online) so that they can gain insights, alter perspectives, be challenged on current thinking, and engage in deep inquiries. A rich environment allows for student choice in texts of all kinds and in responses generated by those texts. The class benefits from the personal views and knowledge that individuals bring to the issues being explored.

Incorporating response activities into the classroom provides students with opportunities to explore issues that are relevant to their lives, to become more articulate in their arguments, and to discuss complex ideas with growing confidence. They have reasons for reflecting on and revising thoughts and opinions; they come to understand the need to inform and persuade; they begin to grasp the requirements of different audiences and to articulate and rethink what they want to express. Each reader also needs to realize that others reading the same text may find different ideas in it and make different connections to it. Through discussion and analysis, readers absorb the diversity of meanings their classmates have built with the text, and this modifies and develops their understanding of the meanings they themselves may have made. Sharing text experiences helps students come to know how they read, how they listen, how they make meaning, and what their own perspectives are. By sharing meanings with others, they build a stronger and bigger world for themselves.

A Motivating New Form of Literacy: Graphic Texts

Being multimodal, graphic texts represent new, contemporary forms of print and visual literacy, and can motivate some readers to read words and images with stronger comprehension. The illustrations and designs support the reading of these books in print and on screen, and students often make greater connections to media experiences in school and at home. These books are highly visual, incorporating art, design, and graphics in support of the printed text. Graphic stories — fiction and nonfiction selections, written and drawn by graphic artists — involve young readers in texts that represent new contemporary forms of literacy that can motivate them to read the words and images with confidence.

Responding in the Content Areas

Today, the quality of nonfiction texts for students has risen dramatically, and many of these serve as an introduction to a vast array of topics. Youngsters are fascinated by the many aspects of the world around them, including the people in communities familiar or strange, the stories of heroes, the habits and habitats of animals, the presence of dinosaurs, and the explanations of scientific wonders. Many nonfiction texts today offer significant literacy experiences because they represent some of our most important historical, geographical, scientific, and artistic moments through time. We need to consider our work with nonfiction texts as opportunities for developing literacy skills and for making connections in a response-based classroom.

We can begin to include the different response modes as relevant instructional tools in every subject discipline, from designing graphic maps to documenting a science experiment with words and diagrams. Redefining the meaning of *text* has altered how we can approach our models of instruction in all subjects. Through their responses to texts concerned with information, opinion, and exposition, students can take the lead in constructing the knowledge they need, and have discovered or considered, and integrate that learning into their own developing understanding.

In the following special contribution, Karen Grose discusses the Internet as text.

THE INTERNET AS TEXT

Karen Grose

Karen Grose is vice-president, Digital Education, for TV Ontario (TVO), the public television authority for the province.

Teachers and school leaders know that, although the fundamental skills of reading, writing, and mathematics remain the foundation of learning, this century's explosion of technology has extended our understanding of what it means to be literate. Networked digital technologies have made communication more complex. Students today have the ability to share and to express themselves through a wide range of technological tools, anytime, anywhere, through any preferred learning modality. All learners need a variety of multi-faceted thinking skills to navigate digital, multimodal text and media-laden environments to effectively interpret huge volumes of new information; to use oral and written language to persuasively communicate, promote, and advance their ideas; and to think critically about language in particular contexts to succeed in learning, work, and life.

Jenkins, Henry. 2009. *Education for the 21st Century*. Cambridge, MA: MIT Press.

Technology has the potential to make literacy an interactive, collaborative experience. Jenkins (2009) explains, "Participatory culture shifts the focus of literacy from one of individual expression to community involvement" (p. 4). Discussions in the educational community acknowledge that the path forward to better support outcomes for all students requires a balance between the effective evidence-based practices already widely understood as drivers to improve student achievement and new learner-centric pedagogies, structures, and practices supported by technologies that deepen learning, increase engagement, and make learning relevant and authentic.

LITERACY IN TODAY'S LEARNING ENVIRONMENT

What does this mean to transforming literacy for K to 12 students? Although a wide array of media existed before the 21st century, technology today has expanded the potential for learning in both time and space. With collaborative technologies that support distributed learning now commonplace, information literacy, which includes digital collaboration, and the process of collective knowledge-building using digital media have significantly changed what is seen as fundamental knowledge. The development of fundamental literacy and the age-old 6 C skills of critical thinking, collaboration, communication, creativity, character education, and citizenship (Fullan 2013) can be supported in today's technology-rich context through a wide array of modalities that result in a more dynamic and outward-reaching participatory learning culture.

Regardless of innovation or ingenuity, the effectiveness of any technological tool is dependent on its ability to address educational need. Although teachers and school leaders know students can be more engaged in their learning using technological tools to support learning, a solid longitudinal body of research that proves to teachers that technology adds value to learning has not yet been amassed. What is clear in academic research is that effective teaching and instruction directly affect student achievement and that the quality of a school system rests on the quality of its teachers (Hattie 2011; Mourshed, Chijioke, and Barber 2010). To support knowledge-building communities that extend and deepen literacy learning today, the use of technology in classrooms will be successful only when technology is effectively used as a tool to support sound pedagogical practices, and the tools used are connected to authentic teaching and learning.

HOW MIGHT TECHNOLOGY SUPPORT LITERACY IN SCHOOLS TODAY?

Leaving behind cultures where students were passive consumers of knowledge, and instead, embracing participatory cultures of learning where thinking is visible, literacy is now forward-focused. What's more, the embedding of 21st century technologies has placed new demands on teachers and school leaders. How might these realities be addressed?

Teachers and school leaders can support the development of critical 21st century literacy skills and ICT (information and communication technologies) competencies by

- creating knowledge-building communities that collaboratively explore and share new knowledge, expose students to a diversity of thought, and extend and enrich meaning making, thereby enhancing critical thinking and deepening understandings;
- encouraging students to use different kinds of media to step into "global conversations" to share information and ideas and to collaborate with multiple audiences to solve problems;
- providing platforms to reflect interactively on reading with others who have shared the same text to deepen a growing understanding of the text, and to help students to reflect collaboratively on their work with others, thereby identifying what they know and what they don't understand;

Fullan, Michael. 2013. *Great to Excellent: Launching the Next Stage of Ontario's Education Agenda*. http://www.edu.gov.on.ca/eng/document/reports/fullan.html.

Hattie, John. 2011. *Visible Learning for Teachers: Maximizing Impact on Learning*. London, UK: Routledge.

Mourshed, Mona, Chinezi Chijioke, and Michael Barber. 2010. *How the World's Most Improved School Systems Keep Getting Better*. London, UK: McKinsey and Company. http://mckinseyonsociety.com/how-the-worlds-most-improved-school-systems-keep-getting-better.

Global conversations are conversations that connect the readers to a larger framework, outside and beyond their own situations. As Freire said, "Reading the word, reading the world."

- providing virtual spaces for book clubs that help build communities of readers;
- providing broader participatory environments where students engage in dialogue, collaboration, and inquiry and where they feel like their voices matter, thereby encouraging ownership in the reading and writing process;
- ensuring that there is shared ownership for learning by providing authentic opportunities for students to learn from and with each other, and for educators to learn from and with students; and
- focusing learning opportunities regarding digital citizenship and respectful participation.

Incorporating Reading Strategies inside Student Responses

We can find hundreds of texts and articles written over the last decades that list thinking skills for us, from Bloom's taxonomy to every contemporary college text on reading. But for me, the turnaround came in the early 1970s with James Moffett's *Student-Centered Language Arts and Reading, K–12*, when Moffett explained how these thinking processes had been misappropriated by educators and labeled only as "reading skills." His rethinking of these processes leads directly into our use today of the word *text* as something more inclusive than only printed texts.

What's vital to students' growth as readers, listeners, and viewers

Thinking operations occur within and in our responses to all the texts we experience in our lives, as, for example, conversations, films, books, magazines, computer texts, and DVDs. Nevertheless, helping students to become aware of the relationship between thought and print in the texts they meet is vital to their growth as readers. A friend, about to embark on a canoeing trip in the north, asked his father if he knew someone who could accompany them — someone who could "read rivers." There are many literacies, including rivers, and they all involve "reading" to find one's way.

Readers need to construct and, as necessary, repair meaning as they proceed. Doing this involves going back and salvaging what they can, clarifying their thinking, noticing when they lose focus, rereading to enhance understanding, reading ahead to clarify meaning, questioning the text, disagreeing with information or logic, identifying and articulating what is confusing or puzzling about the text, drawing inferences, determining what is important, and synthesizing their new learning. These strategies are all involved with students engaging in response activities that continue the inquiry into the text and the emerging connections. Responses themselves become texts, and the reading/thinking strategies continue to support meaning making for both the responders and the other students who may be interpreting their work: the research, the narrative, the PowerPoint presentation, the film, or the poem.

How to help students recognize and develop connections

Reading is an act, and when we are engaged in it, connections are occurring constantly and simultaneously. We recall personal experiences, summarize what has happened so far, synthesize information and add it to our constantly expanding mental storehouse, analyze and challenge the author's ideas, and change the organizational schema of our minds. Nonetheless, making connections with what we read is a complex process.

Reading Strategies

Ministries of education and school districts are now incorporating the following processes as strategies for how readers make sense of a text:
- connecting to self, texts, and the world;
- making inferences;
- visualizing the text;
- determining and prioritizing ideas;
- summarizing the text;
- analyzing the text;
- synthesizing information.

Our main goal as literacy teachers must be to help students build bridges between the ideas in the text and in their own lives, helping them to access the prior knowledge that is relevant to making meaning with the text, the information that the brain has retained and remembered, sometimes accompanied by emotional responses or visual images. When we help students enhance their reading by activating their own connections, we offer them a reading strategy for life.

Use text sets to foster text-to-text connections. We can help students begin to recognize text-to-text connections by selecting particular text sets to be used during reading times or as responses to a text: books related by common themes or writing styles; books, films, or Internet sites about the same events or content; several books by the same author or from a particular genre; different versions of the same story; or relevant research that deepens understanding. Comparisons and contrasts offer us a simple means of noting text-to-text connections.

Promote text-to-world connections through response. In my own work in the teaching of reading strategies, I am seldom satisfied unless the learning stretches outside the classroom lives of the students, connecting their texts to bigger world issues so that perspectives and assumptions are challenged or altered. Paulo Freire coined the expression "reading the word, reading the world." Somehow, when we experience powerful, significant texts and then have opportunities to respond with our puzzlements, interpretations, and explorations, we travel outside ourselves, exploring what lies beyond our immediate neighborhood, extending our vision, and encouraging our personal meaning-making.

Ask students organic questions. As a teacher, I have questions to ask, but they will grow from conversations with the students, from the honest revelations of the students' own concerns, as I strive to guide them into deeper and more subtle interpretations of a text. Just as I would in talk with peers during a book-club session, I try to ask questions driven by our inquiring dialogue, based on my listening to their interactions rather than on my own scripted agenda. I want students to engage in thoughtful consideration about the text and its connections to their lives, not struggle to find the responses they think I want. I like the description Gay Su Pinnell and Irene Fountas give in *Guiding Readers and Writers* for using this strategy: "The teacher's questions are a light scaffold that helps students examine text in new ways" (p. 294).

Making inferences

As readers or viewers, we make inferences when we go beyond the literal meaning of the text — whether it is a film, a conversation, a speech, or a book — and begin to examine the implied meanings, reading between the lines to hypothesize the "understory." When we engage with a text, the meaning-making imperative drives us to infer; we struggle to make sense, searching our minds to explain what isn't on the page or screen, building theories that are more than just the words. We conjecture while we are "reading," the information accrues, and our ideas are modified, changed, or expanded as this new text enters the constructs in our brain.

Predictions are inferences that are usually confirmed or altered, but most inferences are open-ended, unresolved, adding to the matrix of our connections. Often, we need to respond and express our thoughts, sometimes with others, to further explore these ideas and to become more adept at recognizing the need for digging deeply inside the text. In subsequent chapters, you will see examples of students using inferring to move inside the lines of a text as they "dig" for understanding.

The Role of Published Programs
Lists of predigested and impersonal comprehension questions are a less significant part of effective classroom teaching today; however, published programs may offer teachers ideas for giving students thoughtful and deepening literacy strategies, for developing book sets to increase the reading repertoires of the students, or for including significant background information to support the text.

Pinnell, Gay Su, and Irene Fountas. 2000. *Guiding Readers and Writers.* Portsmouth, NH: Heinemann.

Visualizing the text

When we read, we create pictures of what the print suggests, making movies in our heads. And these images are personal, each one of us building a visual world unlike any other. Reading words causes us to see pictures, which is understandable since words are only symbols, a code for capturing ideas and feelings.

Several classrooms described in the following chapters incorporate activities that explore the meanings suggested by an artist's illustration, an effective means of demonstrating visualization and the need to reconsider our thoughts as we learn more. Students often come to recognize their own visualization strengths as they represent their emerging and growing understandings through media explorations such as drawing and painting, creating tableaux, and sculpting.

Determining and prioritizing ideas

Students may have been noting details and main ideas, writing them down in notebooks and highlighting them in their textbooks, yet still be unable to remember what they were trying to understand. What we use in constructing meaning are the pieces of information that add to our growing understanding of what we want to find out or are ready to experience. These are details we can't do without — they are pieces of the puzzle necessary for creating the complete picture. Engaging in a response project may offer the students another look at the selection and its ideas, discovering what to remember, what to take away, what to disregard, or what matters most.

Summarizing the text

Summarizing is an organizing and reorganizing strategy that allows us to categorize and classify the information we are gathering as readers, so that we can add it to our storehouse of knowledge and memory. We need to constantly connect to the new information we garner from the text, and to find a way of making sense of it so that we can assimilate it into our ever-developing construct of knowledge. Response activities that ask us to consider the selection — its central ideas, its organizational patterns, the argument — help us to rethink our summaries thus far, as we interpret and express our emerging thoughts.

Analyzing the text

Through involving and reflective responses, we can help students discover the underlying organization, the elements that identify the genre, the format of the selection (including graphic support), and the overall effect of the work. For me, these are opportunities for guiding readers into a deeper awareness of the text, the author's techniques, and their own developing interpretations. We want them to think critically about the issues they encounter, and analyzing texts through affective and effective responses can move them into stronger patterns of understanding how texts work.

Synthesizing information from the text

When we synthesize, we move from recounting the new information into rethinking our own constructs of the ideas in the text. We synthesize our new learning in order to consider the big ideas that affect our lives. We want to develop readers who construct meaning by interpreting the content and responding personally to what they have "read."

Demonstrating literacy strategies

As teachers, we can contribute to the sense of community by reading aloud to students, often choosing materials they normally would not experience. As we read aloud and think aloud in classroom demonstrations with a common text, we can share our own reading strategies. Students can see how we construct meaning in a variety of ways with different types of texts: how we teachers still grow as readers.

We can constantly look for texts to share with students in other ways, as well. I might scan a selection to use on the data projector, tape a piece to the chalkboard, or make copies for students to read and highlight. I have these teaching tools for illustrating so many aspects of how I make my own meaning with these types of texts; at the same time, the students meet selections they might not notice on their own. They also come to see that literacy is an everyday occurrence in our lives.

When we think out loud in our demonstrations as we read, we make the processing of ideas visible to our students, so that they see how we handle a piece of text either as a reader or as a writer. During these brief *think-aloud and show sessions*, we can reveal what we think before we read, while we read, and after we read. When students have opportunities to see our response processes in action, they may be able to apply similar strategies in their own work.

Having considered general approaches to creating a response-based classroom, we will now see how various response-based classrooms addressed the selchie folktale through the 10 modes of our response repertoire. The accounts of these classroom experiences are presented according to the response modes they most represent, and you will notice that responses quickly become multimodal in an interactive and engaged classroom.

CHAPTER 3

Text Talk

Text talk is an essential element of a response repertoire. It is the first of 10 response modes through which we will explore how students have made meaning of the selchie folktale in various ways and classes. First, though, let's consider briefly the transformative nature of response modes.

The Transformative Nature of Response Modes

Within each of the 10 response modes identified (see the margin list), there will be different forms that students can employ in constructing, expressing, and representing their ideas about what they have read, seen, or heard. The very act of responding will often change their understanding and perceptions of the text they have encountered. As the maxim goes: *We may not understand what we have said until someone tells us what they think we have said.* Students need to consider their initial responses, to rethink their ideas, to refine their understandings, to articulate their initial thoughts and hear them interpreted by others, to explore their reactions to a text, and discover new perceptions and meaning through their response activities.

Responses generate other responses, and different modes may be needed to hold new concepts and directions that emerge as students begin working within one mode. In this chapter and the nine chapters that follow, you will observe how students may begin with one response mode and move into other related and connected modes. For example, a heated discussion can transform into written opinions or a serious debate; the retelling of a story may cause students to express in paint their feelings about the events that occurred; an inquiry may morph into a seminar or panel where the findings are shared in a formal manner.

Response activities are self-generating and transformative. They accrue with the interest and engagement of individuals and of the class as a whole. We need to value the energy and attention that students devote to the world of meaning making negotiated through effective and affective responses.

Children as text makers

We know that the students' engagement with text can be extended and deepened through response activities and that these can incorporate the multimodal forms that surround the children in their lives as they explore the author's content, structure, and forms, interpreting, constructing, and representing their own ideas and emotions in a variety of modes. The children then become the *text makers*, expressing and sharing their constructs with others so that their texts beget other texts. We might call these new forms "*informal* children's literature," as we recognize the power of the peer creation as a force for literacy in the classroom. Children are then developing an awareness of how different texts work, from the inside out, learning that all the new forms are a valuable resource in developing their own interpretations, narratives, new-found information, or word play. After all, a crayon is a technological tool, whether it be a Crayola or a mouse-driven color brush on screen.

Talking Their Way into Meaning

Talk is a bridge that helps students explore relationships that arise between what they know and what they are coming to know. It can help them make sense out loud as they come to grips with new ideas and understanding emerging from the texts they are experiencing.

Dialogic, or interactive, talk involves peer talk — the collective, building on ideas of others. It encompasses dialogue, conversation, and reciprocal listening; use of appropriate language and register; an awareness of the social conventions of talk; and a willingness to rethink and revise after listening to others. With the advent of technology, new forms of talk can affect what happens in our classrooms.

With *digital talk*, the form, the technical format, the audience, and the immediate response time characteristic of interacting through technology are significant factors in determining what we say, to whom we say it, and how we say it. So, what impact will digital talk have on our students' abilities to communicate and interact with others? How can we incorporate digital talk in our classrooms, alongside face-to-face interaction? We will need to consider the effect of electronic communication modes on how students are responding to texts and talking to one another and to the world.

Facilitating discussion and conversation as response

We can organize our talk time to encourage response in a variety of ways:

- We can share a common text, and then the students can begin to offer their comments and puzzlements, joining in the conversation with different views or explanations. This spontaneous talk time can initiate other activities that the students can move into or select, and they have the class conversation as stepping-stones to other modes of expression. Sometimes, we can scribe their ideas onto a chart or on screen, and these points can prompt new explorations by groups of students or individuals.
- Students need time to reflect on a text and formulate their ideas before they discuss them with others. We can encourage them to record their responses to a text in their journals as a preparatory step to discussing them in peer and group situations. The act of recording a response may increase students' comfort level at later stages when sharing their ideas.
- Depending on the nature of the discussion, ideas stemming from small-group discussions can be shared among classmates. This form of sharing can be done by jigsaw grouping, where each student, in a small group, takes a number from 1 to 4. Students with the same number form a second group. New group members take turns sharing their previous group's discussion. It is helpful to tape and record some of the discussion, both for you as teacher to analyze and for students to read and reflect on their contributions.
- Literature circles allow students to engage in authentic book talk. As they discuss aspects of their reading, including predictions, perceptions, and

In *Interactive Think-Alouds,* Lori Oczkus offers ideas for demonstrating with and engaging students in exploring texts in a variety of ways that highlight thinking and literacy strategies with all types of texts.

responses, students understand what they have read at a deep level and can relate their reading to their own lives and prior knowledge. They can discuss a variety of factors, including elements of plot, language devices, setting, and characters; how the text relates to another they have read; stylistic details; and the work of any illustrator. They can listen to the wide-ranging opinions of their peers and witness first-hand how the experience of literature is personal.

- Working in these small groups can provide students with opportunities for being heard, for expressing their individual responses to the text they are reading, for having their feelings and ideas validated, and for changing opinions and viewpoints.
- Harvey Daniels, whose writings have helped us move forward, has rethought the process of small-group text discussions in *Literature Circles: Voice and Choice in Book Clubs and Reading Groups*. He notes that students who have difficulty reading a text can still enter the group discussion if they have been able to use technology that offers assisted reading support. (Many excellent programs are available online or licensed to school districts.)
- Every teacher can be a member of a book club or a literature circle simply by reading a novel that a group of students are reading and entering the conversation about the text. A teacher can enter as a listener and sometimes as a contributor who grows in personal understanding through the contributions of other book club members.
- We can also frame literacy journeys with texts in language arts or in other curriculum subjects as inquiries where students pursue understanding, making connections with what others are thinking, as different class members engage in discussion. Sometimes, the discussion will occur in a large group, sometimes in small groups or with a partner. The interplay among members of the literacy community enables and engenders the processes of meaning making.

Introduction to Demonstrations of Talk Responses

The six articles that follow are about classroom experiences with text talk that grew from my visits with teachers who took part in our wide-scale Selchie Project. The students working with this response mode range from children in Grades 1 and 2 to young adolescents in Grades 9 and 10. Yet you will find similar connections to the themes in all of their responses about the selchie people, from raising questions about the strange events of their story to discussing and debating in role the ethical behavior of the characters, from talking about the various interpretations of reading lines from a poem to having intense conversations through the power of iPads. Talk can be the precursor to so many other response modes, as students clarify and expand their understanding of texts before moving forward with other ways of representing ideas and feelings. We talk to learn.

QUESTIONING THE TEXT

David Booth with Stephanie Perry, Jen Hart, and Sabine Dietz

We read because we are curious about what we will find; we keep reading because of the questions that continue to fill our reading minds. Of course, readers ask questions before they read, as they read, and when they are finished reading. As we become engaged with a text, questions keep popping up, questions that propel us to predict what will happen next, to challenge the author, to wonder about the context for what is happening, to fit the new information into our world picture. We seek to rectify our confusion, filling in missing details, trying to fit into a pattern all the bits and pieces that float around our sphere of meaning making. We continue to read because the author has stirred our curiosity, and constant self-questioning causes us to interact with the text, consciously and subconsciously. As we read on, our questions may change, and the answers we seek may lie outside the print.

THE LURE OF CONFUSION

Often, our most limited readers ask themselves the fewest questions as they read; instead, they wait for us to interrogate them when they have finished what for them is the disenfranchising ritual of reading. They have not learned that confusion is allowed as we read, that, in fact, authors count on it in order to build the dynamic that compels us to continue reading. As students grow in their ability to self-question, their understanding of how authors think and of how meaning makers work increases.

The three demonstrations that follow represent students at Crescent Town Public School, Toronto, who responded with their own questions.

1. SEASHELL ARTIFACTS

The first demonstration happened in Stephanie Perry's class of students with special needs. The class worked with a different selchie story, *The Seal Mother*, by Mordicai Gerstein.

I visited Stephanie Perry's class as a storyteller to share a version of the selchie tales. Working with the picture book *The Boy Who Lived with the Seals* by Rafe Martin, I showed the pictures as I read the story to the students. Their subsequent responses centered on whether the story was fact or fiction, since they had been previously concerned with this issue. I asked them to vote with the raising of hands as to which category they felt the story fitted, and they all voted for fiction. During the ensuing conversation, the students shared the reasons for their choice, commenting on several facts that they felt proved their point.

I then presented each child with a white seashell and said I had picked the shells up from a beach close to where the seal-boy story had taken place. I wondered aloud if this might change their minds about the reality of the tale, and a girl said that she had seen porpoises at Sea World and sometimes they had seemed human. But one boy insisted, "The story is fiction, but a lot of kids do leave home."

This class had discussed the tale with intense concentration and left holding their shells and talking to each other about the experience. They reminded me once again that every child deserves a chance to engage in meaningful conversations about things that matter and that the story must become the child's to own. A shell can be a text, holding inside itself another story.

2. QUESTIONS ARISING FROM THE STORY

The second demonstration I outline took place in Jen Hart's Grade 1 class at Crescent Town Public School in Toronto.

I visited the Grade 1 class as part of the school's participation in the Selchie Project. The class had previously experienced *The Seal Mother* by Mordicai Gerstein so I read *The Boy Who Lived with the Seals* by Rafe Martin, an Indigenous people's telling of a similar legend. After the experience of the story and the sharing of David Shannon's images in the book, the students peppered me with their puzzlements and comments, including some that connected to the other story they had heard. Further discussion resulted. This summary reveals their concerns, some expressed as questions, some as statements.

"I can't believe the boy would live in the water because he would be dead right away." (Yamlak)

"How did the boy breathe in the canoe when he was hidden under the blanket?" (Amna)

"A boy would need an oxygen tank under water." (Naail)

"If he is a human, how will he die, in the water, or in a grave?" (Sameer)

"Why did he want to live with the seals?" (Ahnaf)

"I have a text-to-text connection: both stories have a mom, a dad, and a boy." (Shnehasish)

"I go to swimming classes and I do not sink. Did he take swimming class?" (Tharnika)

"I want to know why the boy did not float when he fell into the water, instead of diving down, down?" (Muntahar)

"How could the boy survive under water because there are a lot of sharks?" (Rohith)

"Does the boy like the seals better than his parents?" (Sienna)

3. "BIG IDEA" QUESTIONS

This demonstration occurred in Sabine Dietz's Grade 4 class, also at Crescent Town Public School in Toronto. The class worked with a different selchie story, *The Seal Mother*, by Mordicai Gerstein.

In this Grade 4 class, the teacher uses the "big idea" concept with her students as part of every lesson. The students offer their questions, and as the work progresses, they present answers to them, along with new queries that have arisen. The students attach sticky notes to the main chart in a different color as they work through the lesson under these three categories:

- Our Fierce Wonderings
- Our Answers to Our Wonderings [inferred and researched]
- Further Wonderings

I was impressed with this approach, and the following list, selected from their sticky note submissions, demonstrates their thoughts after engaging with the story. The students wonder about the nature of human and seal, about the construct of the story, about what might happen next, about the author's choices of topics — all the kinds of questions that I would hope readers of this tale would ponder, regardless of age.

"What is Midsummer's Eve? Where is it celebrated?" (Shakila)

"How could a seal mother give birth to a human baby?" (Prottoy)

"I wonder how Andrew climbed down to the cave in the story?" (Amra)

"Are selchies real seals? Do they really shed their skins?" (Zahra and Ishtiaque)

"Why seven years — why not less, why not more?" (Samanta)

"Is the storyteller Andrew himself or his son?" (Mahdi)

"Did Andrew ever see his mother after he found her seal skin?" (Ifti)

"I wonder why the author chose the selchie as his book. Why do the selchies go into their old skins when they return to the sea?" (Ryan)

"What is phosphorus?" (Mahdi)

"Why did the man marry a seal? And why did he play the fiddle?"
(Kabeer)
"Did Andrew feel bad when his mother turned into a seal? Did
the fisherman marry another woman after the seal wife left?"
(Shydharta)

BUILDING STORY CONNECTIONS

David Booth and Bob Barton

Bob Barton is a master storyteller. In his book *Story Works* (which I co-author), he demonstrates his strategies for telling stories and suggests ways to help students draw upon their own lives to develop their personal stories.

Story talk with the whole class presents a public forum for shared common experiences related to story. It allows for reflective talk after other response modes have been explored. Students can talk about the pictorial representations, the writing, the drama, the research, and so forth. The talk may focus on the story meanings or on the storyteller, on the students' identification with the story, on the stories within the story, on the background information, on the conflict, the resolution, the use of language, the difficulty of idiom, the word choice, the sentence structure, the style. It is important that, at times, the story talk be focused on the story itself, whether at the beginning of story talk, or as a summary or reflection of the dialogue. The students may leave the story in order to understand it better, but they should return to see its reflection in the new learning, the new meaning that has grown from the talk.

A TALE OF TRUST AND HONOR

We were asked to address two Grade 6 classes and their parents in a rural Canadian community for the students' graduation ceremony. We chose to read Katherine Paterson's *The Crane Wife*, a beautiful reworking of an old Japanese folktale. *The Crane Wife* is often included with selchie tales in discussions of folk themes of transformation, and in our Selchie Project, it served as a parallel story.

The Crane Wife is a story of a poor man who saves the life of a wounded crane and later is rewarded when he marries a young woman. Their happiness wanes as their poverty grows, and she offers to weave for him cloth to sell at market, on the condition that he does not watch her as she works. He agrees, and the beautiful cloth is sold for a handsome sum. Of course, the husband requests that she once again weave the cloth, and she consents. Upon his neighbors' urging, he orders her to work her magic a third time, but this time he slides the door open and sees a crane ripping out her feathers in order to weave. She sees him and flies away, never to return. For us, it is a tale of trust and honor, and we felt it suitable for young people about to enter junior-high school.

AN INQUIRY INTO CLOTH

After we had read the story, we asked the students for their comments and feelings about the man or the crane wife. One girl asked, "How do you weave cloth?" We briefly described the process and attempted to refocus the discussion, but other students interrupted our progress with other questions and concerns about the making of cloth.

We realized that for these students at this time *The Crane Wife* is a story of weaving. We asked them to look at the labels in their shirts and sweaters for the place of origin of the cloth and then on the chalkboard listed all the countries they found. After calling out over 40 locales, the class asked why Canada wasn't represented on any of the labels. This issue caused them to search further — their pants, skirts, even underwear. We noticed that the parents were joining in the quest, and, in fact, everyone was looking at each other's clothes for the honor of their country. At last, a small voice cried out, "In my running shoe, I found it: 'Made in Canada'!" All the people, young and old, applauded with a standing ovation as the two of us left the room.

STUDENTS SETTING THE COURSE OF TALK

The students had directed the journey — we were only guides along the route. We had begun with a theme that held little interest for the students, and we were forced to abandon it during the session. In a regular classroom setting, we could perhaps bring the talk around to why, in Japanese folklore, weaving held such a prominent place or why the supernatural character was the one who spun cloth. Nonetheless, the students should decide how to begin the story talk, and their contributions should help us develop the learning areas.

GROUP TALK USING IPADS

Lynda Marshall

My all-girls Grade 10 Applied English class had just finished a writing assignment, in which I challenged them to dig down and write at a deeper level than they had ever done before. The assignment was a personal narrative on the topic of their choice. Since this undertaking was successful, I decided to challenge them to put on their scuba suits and dive into reading a text the same way they had just dived into telling their stories. The selchie folklore was the perfect vehicle for this.

After going online and doing more research on selchie folklore, I introduced the reading by sharing topical information, such as where the folklore originated and why people possibly believed in such tales. I did not explain what a selchie was, nor did I go into details of the story itself.

LESSON 1: SELF-DIRECTED DISCUSSION

I put the class into groups of three and gave each group one prose story, one ballad, and one copy of background information about selchies. I also gave each group an iPad. I sent them out to a private location to complete a certain task.

The task was outlined as follows.

First task: Each group was to read the story first, then discuss it, taping their conversation with the iPad. Members were to orally share what they thought the reading was about, what seemed to be happening, and what their opinions, concerns, and questions were.

Second task: Next, they were to read the ballad (some read silently, some read aloud). They were to audiotape this discussion, as well, filling in any "holes" they could, comparing and contrasting the two selections, asking new or additional questions, and explaining their understanding of the ballad.

Third task: Finally, the students were to read the background information provided and once more, tape the discussion. Some of the questions were answered, some understandings were made clearer, and some insights that were formerly nonexistent were made.

When we reconvened in the classroom, the girls arrived with Celtic music playing. The music was intended as a cue to further deepen understanding. Most of them responded to it immediately.

Today, we could use images from the Internet to open discussions, asking which picture students would choose as the basis for writing a variation on the tale. There are at least five picture-book versions of "The Crane Wife." A generic version of "The Crane Wife" can be found at http://cherylkirknoll.com/cranewifeloss.html.

Lynda Marshall describes working with a Grade 10 class at Widdifield Secondary School, in North Bay, Ontario. As you read the comments of the students transcribed from iPad-captured conversations, you will see the changes in understanding that group members brought to the discussion, extending everyone's interpretation of the tale. Meaning accrues over time through engaged talk.

Lynda writes, "I also wanted to see whether the girls would use the iPads to look up *selchies* or other vocabulary they did not know, such as *bairns*, from the ballad, or images to help deepen their understanding of this text. Some did, and some did not."

I took the iPads home and listened to all of the discussions, compiling the ideas, thoughts, questions, and insights. (See the transcripts below.)

The next day I went over these discussion points with the whole class and had an interesting, sometimes hilarious, discussion without adding my own ideas or input. Many intriguing questions and *aha* moments happened here.

The following comments are compiled points from iPad audio-recorded conversations.

FIRST TASK: READING AND DISCUSSING THE STORY

Group #1:
"I think a man went to a cave and heard laughter."
"Took a seal's skin."
"Or a woman's skin?"
"Then the man found a woman weeping and he did not know she was really a seal."
"He did not know it was her skin that he had taken."
"They got married and had seven kids."
"She also had seven kids in the sea."
"I guess her kids will all turn into seals when they die."

Group #2:
"It sounds like an exorcism, but in a good way."
"Yah, it is like the positive side of exorcism."
"The woman is possessed by the seal and the man sets her free by taking her skin."

Group #3:
"Someone stole someone's skin?"
"The guy took the skin from the seal."
"He made her his sex slave."
"But maybe they had a good marriage."
"But she goes back to the ocean because she likes it better than she likes her husband."

SECOND TASK: COMPARING AND CONTRASTING PROSE STORY AND BALLAD

Group #1:
"Why would she throw them jelly fish?"
"Maybe she wanted to shock them (electricity kind of shock)."
"Perhaps the jellyfish are symbolic of something."
"Yah, but symbolic of what?"
"He should not have left the key under the pillow."
"She could have escaped any time, but decided not to."
"She stuck around to have 'bairns.' "
"This is just weird . . . why would anyone drag a seal skin home?"
"I would rather have a seal than a boyfriend!"
"I kissed a walrus once!"
"Some random guy just took a woman to be his wife."
"Once she got away she never came back to him."

"I know! . . . this is a story of BETRAYAL. She must have found out that it was him who stole her skin."

"This makes me think of Ariel, the mermaid."

Group #2:

"If they eat seal meat, they would be eating their mother."

"Kids were supernatural."

"Does this mean they have super-powers?"

"They must if they can change from a human to a seal, then back again."

Group #3:

"That woman just found her skin and left all her children."

"What a terrible mother!"

"But she had others in the sea."

"Other what?"

"Children. Why should she have to choose? The husband is the one who took away her choices."

THIRD TASK: READING BACKGROUND INFORMATION AND TAPING THE DISCUSSION

Group #1:

"The woman is trapped on land."

"She eventually is able to go back to the sea."

"She never returns to land though, because she is afraid to be trapped again, forever."

"This is a story of a very selfish man."

"No consideration of her feelings."

Group #2:

"If there are seal girls and seal boys, why don't they just get together instead of being stolen by humans?"

"The seal tossing fish is showing that she cares and wants to provide for her human children."

"The shells are like an offering of some kind."

"I wonder what the supernatural son thing means."

"Maybe because the wife is not really human, the sons are not human either."

"Maybe the son can also change into a seal."

Group #3:

"I read here that to entice a male selchie, one has to cry tears in the ocean."

"It is obviously harder to steal a male selchie than to steal a female."

"This just shows one more case of history where the women are weak and helpless."

"The male seals can decide whether to come ashore if they want to, but the women are taken — they have no choice."

"The seal skin is like clothing . . ."

"Perhaps it represents the rape of the female."

"I think the skin is symbolic of the man walking away or leading the way and having total control over the woman."

LESSON 2: CHOOSING AND MAKING A SMALL-GROUP RESPONSE

Students were provided with the following response options:

- Create a *Comic Life* book of seal images and interactions, indicating human qualities seals possess.
- Write a poem or interior monologue as the "wife" in the story.
- Create a painting or illustration to convey your understanding of the feelings and emotions captured in this tale.
- Interview the husband and the wife in such a way as to convey their differing points of view and impressions of events. You can be a villager, the oldest child, a researcher, or another person of your choice.
- Put one person in your group on the "hot seat" and pretend you are villagers questioning (accusing?) the husband as to where the mother of his children has gone.
- Research the SELKIES, NORSE MERMAIDS, and SEALS, and create a Prezi or a PowerPoint to share your information. Connect this research directly to your group's reading.

I then had the students choose from the assignment sheet, as a group, one task they could do together to deepen their understanding and convey that understanding to the rest of the class through an informal presentation.

THREE CREATIVE RESPONSES

One group chose to write poetry, taking on different roles. There were four girls in the group, so one was the husband, one the wife, one the woman as a seal, and one the oldest son. These poems were wonderful. The group presented and talked about how writing the poetry in role made them understand what was happening, what the relationships were, and how the characters felt. This was very "deep" for this group of Applied learners.

OUT WITH A SPLASH

I took her skin
Leaving her no choice.
I married her and
I locked her skin away,
Oh so far away!
Kept the key on me every
   day.
She lay by the window,
   day after day,
Saying she's okay as she
   obeyed.
They said she could not go
   anyway,
'Til today —
She ran away.
Still today,
I see her as I ship away.

SEAL EYES

The next day
I felt even worse,
so I went down to the sea.
There was a seal
that stood out on the
   rocks.
I then realized
it was my mother,
looking out for me.

Another group put the husband on the hot seat and questioned him as villagers on the disappearance of his wife. They thought the man was a "big jerk" before they undertook this small project, but came around somewhat when they understood he really loved his wife and was missing her dearly.

The third group decided to illustrate their understanding. I liked that they took the vantage point from inside the cave, but they clearly did not have the deeper understanding of the text that the poetry writing group did. We had two drawings. The second drawing told the tale in a timeline. It was when this drawing was just completed that the artist said, "Oh, she had seven children! I get it!" Her drawing does not show seven, but she said some of them are hiding in the house! In one frame, the image depicts a woman "sick" in bed; the artist did not realize that she was "homesick" and longing for the sea . . . she took it literally.

LASTING IMPRESSIONS

Overall, the group that did the hot-seat activity understood the most from the beginning, but the group that wrote the poetry really delved into the reading and created understanding in the process of taking on the roles. It was fascinating! They had no idea when they started. This was the group whose comments included such things as "I kissed a walrus once!"

After the short presentations, we went on the iPads to search for images, movies, music, and so on. The girls watched excerpts of one movie that shows the selchie removing her skin.

At the end of it all, some girls were still uncertain about the story, and some were secure. When asked why this was, one student, Faye, said she had a clear understanding because she loves myths and folktales, and this is one more for her to digest. Hallee (the one who thought the woman was "sick") had never really studied or read mythology and found the concept difficult to understand.

They did all agree that they will never be able to look at a seal or photo of a seal again without seeing the woman's eyes looking back at them.

In this feature, teacher Fatma Faraj observes my work with Grade 6 students at her school, Royal Orchard Middle School, in Brampton, Ontario.

CLOSE READING THROUGH CLASS DISCUSSION AND CHORAL SPEAKING

Fatma Faraj

David Booth visited my class to explore a Jane Yolen poem, "The Selchie's Midnight Song," with a group of Grade 6 students selected from my four drama classes. Mr. Booth came into the library and asked them a question, "Would you ever tell a lie?" That hooked the students. "We would never lie," they responded. He listened to a few comments and then handed out copies of the poem.

That's when I got nervous. My students represent so many diverse backgrounds that as soon as I saw the poem he chose to share with them, I had no idea where this lesson would go. Would the students understand the intricate language that Jane Yolen uses? The few words on the page were hard to create instant meaning from, as an educational assistant confirmed after the lesson. She said it took her about 20 minutes to develop meaning from the text.

As the students struggled with the words in the poem, they were free with their interpretations and ideas. They didn't shy away from sharing their ideas. Students, who are traditionally shy, realized that they needed to share their thoughts aloud. Line by line, the students read the words aloud as Mr. Booth pointed and chose students at random.

Now, as this was going on, I had the privilege to watch the students in action, and I began to notice a pattern in how students answered the questions:

- One student put up his hand up incessantly. Mr. Booth returned to him regularly and encouraged him to make connections to stories other than superhero movies. This didn't stop the student. It made him think below the surface of the text, and with that, he began to see the story of a woman trapped in a loveless marriage.
- What about the student who was reading the text literally, word for word? Mr. Booth returned to him regularly, even as the answers took us far from the meaning of the text. The third return was the charm. The student saw something no one had seen: the selchie was trapped, with children she desperately wanted to return to in the sea.
- One student was hesitant to raise her hand, but when her understanding of the story became clearer, she realized she was on the right track and was confident in her responses. She began to participate without hesitation and gave voice to the selchie woman in a way that was heartfelt and true.

Students participated by turning to their friends to confirm and verify their understanding, or by watching and listening to the language. Once the students understood that it was a selchie who had no choice in her life on land and who had children in the sea, they began to discuss the implications of the situation.

Mr. Booth had the students stand to read the poem chorally, line by line; students took turns and eventually, they were asked this question: "Should she leave the man who has kept her from the water and her other children, or should she stay with her children on the land?" This dilemma was difficult to resolve as this woman had been lied to; however, she had children she would be leaving behind. "What would you do?" the students were asked. They were prompted to stand if they believed she should leave and to sit if they thought she should stay. Students were standing and sitting so quickly it was hard to see an answer. Then the students were tasked with this question: "What should the woman do?" Silence, and then the room exploded. Students ran to grab paper and pencils. Some ran to get an iPad to answer the question orally.

AN EXPLOSION OF CHALLENGING IDEAS

Their answers proved that the lesson was not over. Their responses brought forward new and challenging ideas, such as domestic abuse, imprisonment, women's rights, animal rights, and identity. In less than an hour, reading the text had created something bigger than the moment. It made the students think about their understanding of not only the poem but of issues that are faced by women every day, locally and globally.

When students saw me, either in the library or in the hall, they asked when we could continue the drama. The students were still not satisfied that they knew the answers to the questions that had arisen through the discussion.

STUDENT OPINIONS ON THE SELCHIE'S CHOICE

Below are some of the students' responses (written or via the iPad).

Josh wrote: "She had to care for her seal babies instead of her human babies because the man who fell in love with her killed other seals. She didn't like it so she went back to care for her seal babies."

Sophia wrote: "I think the lady seal should have left because the man kept her skin for 7 years and she also had kids in the ocean. The lady seal has the right to go back to her children."

Reuel wrote: "I think that the seal woman should have left because she should have the freedom she deserves and not be forced against her will to stay somewhere she doesn't want to be. She should return to her original seal family and be somewhere she wants to be instead of somewhere she does not want to be."

Jasvineet wrote: "I think she should leave because no one has the right to force someone into doing something. Seal woman also had a family in the sea. She was returning to her true family, to her true husband, to her true kind and to her true home."

Gurleen wrote: "I would be confused but she should go back to the sea because nobody would want to be forced to live in a place where her kind are killed. But the most confusing part is that she has kids on land and in the sea, and no mother could bear to leave her kids and live her life so she would think of every child of hers."

Students were adamant that her husband was a seal hunter and that she was safer on land than in the water.

Aaron wrote: "I think the woman should not leave because now that she left the man will be even more brutal to seals. The man was already a seal hunter and he loved the woman and now that she left him he will search for and kill many seals."

Then Nathan's answer showed that the selchie would face dilemmas, no matter what she did: "I think she should have stayed. Mostly because if she left it would lead to many seals dying. On the other hand if she stayed none of that would happen but she'd be miserable the rest of her life. So honestly I have a mixed opinion on the matter."

Djanee structured her response as a poem, and several of her classmates gathered around her desk as she wrote, impressed with her mode of sharing.

> The point of my view is for all of you to see,
> The huge burden this seal woman carried.
> She had seal children; she had his breed
> For whom she will care.
> Which cry will she bear,
> So frustrated she had to break free,
> Move from this place
> And back to the sea.

INTERPRETING TEXT THROUGH ARGUMENT AND DEBATE

Pina Marchese

Pina Marchese teaches at Archbishop Romero Catholic Secondary School, in Toronto. Here, she reports on my work with her Grade 9 Religion class.

The story "The Seal's Skin" appears on page 145 in this book. It can be found online at www.vikingrune.com/selkies-folktale.

I invited David Booth to come and work with this class. We began the class with a prayer, "Hail Mary full of grace . . .," and then David took over. The following excerpt is a taped conversation and role-play with a group of 23 Grade 9 students in my Religion class.

David: I want to talk about how some stories help other stories. We look at a story to attempt to find out what it's trying to tell us. That's the secret for all stories. My story today is about love and romance, and the truth of what that means for the couple involved. I will distribute the story "The Seal's Skin," and you can read it for yourselves.

Students read the story silently.

David: Everybody has finished the story. Now we can retell the story. You can start, and the next person will jump in. You start as if you are the storyteller. You can begin . . .

Mitchell: So, a man in Iceland is walking along the shore by the sea . . .

Jessica: There was a naked lady there weeping.

David: And why was she weeping?

Tiago: Because she had lost her seal skin.

David: This wasn't a fur coat. To her, what has she lost?

Ricky: She lost herself.

Benjamin: She removed her seal skin. It was her fault. The man took the seal skin.

David: Does it say why she removed her seal skin? Does it say why?

D'Andre: He just took one.

David: So, what do the others all do?

Ricky: They put theirs on and returned to the ocean.

Kole: They were seals.

David: But the reason why she couldn't go back to the sea was . . . she couldn't wear her seal skin. And the term we give to these people who are half-seal and half-human are *selchies*. It could be either Icelandic or Scottish. But can you think of a movie with a similar theme?

Jessica: *The Little Mermaid.*

David: Same focus. What happened to her life once she lost her seal skin and he took it?

Brian: He gave her clothes and they married.

David: And then what happened?

Tiago: They married and had seven children.

David: What does she think about that? For having a life, but not a full life . . . Being trapped on land . . . What did she feel like to be trapped away from home on land?

Kayla: She lost everything.

David: Was she miserable on land? Does it say she adapted?

Augostino: She felt lonely.

David: What happened according to the story?

Travis: She finds the skin.

David: Now she has the chance to leave her husband, her children, leave her life on land after seven years and return to the sea to re-establish herself under water again. She has to make a decision — a choice. What would you choose to do?

Allison: Go back.

Talisha: Go back.

Jessica: I'd go back.

David: What would make her stay?

Pablo: A family.

David: So, to leave that family for the other family under water was a moral decision. The question is, was it the right one? What do you think should happen to the man? The women in this class would go back. Are you boys thinking as the men in a similar situation? The men are without their wives. What do they tell the community? What do you say to your children?

Mitchell: Tell them the truth.

David: Who would tell the truth to the public, the neighbors . . . ? What would you say to them?

D'Andre: I would not tell the truth.

David: Okay, men, stand if you would not tell. (*Eight male students stand. David asks them to take a seat at the front of the class.*) What have you all decided?

Group of Male Students: We wouldn't tell anyone.

David: There's a difference between lying and not telling the truth. I'll ask each one of you: Would you say *nothing* or *something*?

Benjamin: Say nothing.

Tiago: I'd say nothing.

D'Andre: I'd say something. I'd say she went on a leave of absence for work for 10 years. And during those 10 years, I would try to find her.

David: Where would you spend your time looking?

D'Andre: Near water.

David: Because you're a fisherman, you're allowed to do that.

D'Andre: When I find her, I will ask her, *why, why she left?*

David: I forgot to tell you one thing: once a year, these seal people can come to land. Is that when you will tell her?

D'Andre: Yeah . . .

Augostino: Undecided . . .

Tiago: If I had the choice, I would take the skin again.

David: You would commit the crime twice?

Jessica: Oh, no . . .

David: I wonder how many men, in truth, if they had the chance — he has the children, he had no one to help him raise the kids — would commit the crime one more time?

Travis: Undecided. You see, you know how you said that once a year these seals come on land. How would he know which skin belongs to her?

David: It says that once the seal swam close to him, he recognized the characteristics of that seal.

Brian: Undecided . . .

Ricky: Undecided . . .

David: What would change your mind? How about if the man said to her, I'll give you back your skin and you can come and go as you please, whenever you want? Would that help? Would a woman do that? Do you think she'd ever go back?

Jessica: No . . .

David: If you go back, he would give you the choice. She could take the skin in her own room; you can take it when you need it, but you can only become human once a year. But you could see your kids on land. Would you go back?

Talisha: No.

Benjamin: It's her decision.

Benjamin: I don't think she really liked him.

Mitchell: I don't think you can do anything to bring her back. She's going to see her family. She has family in the sea. "I knew I had a family, and I shouldn't have left in the first place."

David: "Now I'm tired and tethered in the village. My son did this . . . your mother and I are old and we can't work anymore . . . we can't change our lives for what he did." Do you have shame?

Mitchell: Of course.

David: Would you do it again?

Mitchell: No.

David: Some of these people would . . .

David asks the men who wouldn't do it again to sit down.

David: What's it like when you're standing by the sea once a year? The full moon comes out, and suddenly you see the seals and the water and you know that one seal you took is imprisoned . . . Would you feel shame? (*David asks the boys in the group sitting at front of class.*) Are you happy you did it? What is your feeling? Is it so complex you don't even know?

Benjamin: How can you have a feeling about this?

David: Would you confess to a priest?

Pablo: Yes.

Tiago: Yes.

David: I need you women to tell me if you told the people under water — your children there, the seal people — that you *forgive* the man for what he did.

Jessica: I don't know.

Talisha: I'd forgive.

Allison: Forgive . . .

D'Andre: I will forgive myself.

The class laughs.

David: And in the end, you have to forgive yourself . . .

D'Andre: Yes.

David: You wish it hadn't happened?

D'Andre: I have no regrets because it made me a better person. That's how I feel.

David: Now, Tiago, I'm not quite sure what you believe. You've come to the church and I'm the priest . . . What is it you'd like to confess?

Tiago: It's bottled up inside me.

David: So you go back once a year to see the seals?

Tiago: Yes.

David: You have come to confession because you're bottled up. What's bottled up?

Tiago: Anger, my children, I don't feel complete, and I want you and God to forgive me.

David: As a priest, I don't know if I could do that. There's a sin you broke not being with humans . . . Are you going to confession or not?

Pablo: Yeah.

David: Are you going to tell?

Pablo: Yeah . . . Father, seven years ago I was on the shoreline at sea. I saw a seal's skin and I took it. She then became my wife. Seven years later she left me and went back to the sea to visit her family. I want her back.

David: So, as a priest, I have to decide whether I could give you God's blessing for what you did. Forgiveness is a gift.

To the women: Do you think she was penalized under the sea? Did she go back to her life easily? Can you go back to your life? Tough, isn't it? (*pause*) I wonder if they believed her. I think the truth is always hard to find. You have to look very deep within to know the truth.

STUDENTS' INDIVIDUAL RESPONSES TO "THE SEAL'S SKIN"

"The truth of the seal's skin story is that you should never take something that does not belong to you. If you do, it will result in bad karma for you in the future. So you should only take things that are rightfully yours and never keep stuff that is not yours. Always return stuff to the rightful owner." (Melody)

"This story is about *forgiving yourself.* We all make mistakes. But once you forgive yourself, your world could move. Nobody is perfect. You have to do what you have to do." (D'Andre)

"The truth is difficult to tell. 'The Seal's Skin' is about a woman who wakes up after she figures out that she is in the wrong place at the wrong time. Life is too short. You have to be yourself and live the life God gave you. If you don't, you will be unhappy. I believe this is why so many people are unhappy. They follow everybody else and not themselves." (Jessica)

"It's hard to tell what the truth is. There's a lot going on. I feel sorry for the man and kids. They are left without a mother. She obviously left because she wasn't happy about something. Nobody just picks up and leaves without a good reason." (Christian)

"I think that the truth of this story is that you should do things in life that you won't regret. When the man steals the skin away from the seal woman, I think he felt remorse for what he had done, and now he has a family with no mother to raise them. If I were the man, I would tell the truth and pray for forgiveness after all of my actions. I would not have done the same thing again because it was wrong. I would also admit my misconduct." (Mitchell)

"My mother always tells me to follow my heart. I think the Seal woman did just that." (Kayla)

"The truth is to learn to be comfortable in your own skin. Everybody is different. We should learn to accept what God gave us." (Jane)

"I think the truth of this story is that you shouldn't lie to people. The truth is all about 'respect.' Without respect, you have nothing. You have to give the guy credit for going to the sea and hoping she'd come back!" (Brian)

"I think the man should have left if she was so miserable. Why make a big deal out of things?" (Ricardo)

"I don't know! What can I say? People leave people all the time. So what!" (Marcia)

HOW GUIDED DIALOGUE ENCOURAGES RETHINKING

Tina Benevides

Tina Benevides' research focuses on the meaning making that can happen as we engage one student in a brief conference. Through careful prompting, students can attend closely to the text, consider their interpretations as they move along, rework their initial thoughts after reading, and make connections to their own worlds. In the following transcripts, Tina works with her two sons — Adam in Grade 5 and Ben in Grade 8 — one at a time in a guided dialogue process with the story "The Seal's Skin."

It is interesting to note the connections each boy makes and the differences in their responses to the same story.

FIRST INTERVIEW

Tina: Why did the husband keep the seal skin locked away in the chest?

Adam: So that the woman couldn't disappear into the sea.

Tina: What happened when she found the key?

Adam: She opened the chest and took out the seal skin and then went back to the sea.

Tina: What does that tell you about taking something that doesn't belong to you?

Adam: You shouldn't do it because it makes people mad.

Tina: Let's think of your grandfather. Do you think he ever fit into Canada or do you think he still longs to go back to Portugal?

Adam: I think he fits in.

Tina: Do you think if he had the key, he would go back?

Adam: I'm not sure. Maybe.

Tina: If you really love someone, should you keep him or her from what they really want to do?

Adam: No.

Tina: Think of your own life. Is there anyone or anything keeping you from being your true self?

Adam: School.

Tina: What is your seal skin?

Adam: Robotics.

Tina: What would you miss though if we took you out of school?

Adam: My friends.

Tina: What did the seal-skin woman miss by not being able to return to the sea?

Adam: Her children.

Tina: Did living in both worlds enrich her?

Adam: Yes.

Tina: So, do you think that it is important to go outside of your comfort zone sometimes to see what you might be missing? What might that mean for you in your life?

Adam: Well, it means that even though I would like to be home-schooled, I might miss out on a lot of opportunities at school. The seal-skin lady would have missed out on being married and living on land with children if the man did not take the seal skin from the cave.

SECOND INTERVIEW

Tina: What did you think about the story of the seal skin?

Ben: I thought it was pretty cool. It obviously is written in kind of old-fashioned English, but it was weird how it was a party of people who were seals, I guess, and since this guy stole a seal skin, he went back to the cave and saw the person naked because she was half-human and half-seal. Then she came home with him.

Tina: Why did she go home with him?

Ben: I guess because she was depressed.

Tina: What did he have of hers?

Ben: The seal skin.

Tina: Okay. She was in the cave with the selchie humans dancing, so what can you assume about the people she was with?

Ben: That they were half-human and half-seal.

Tina: Why couldn't she go back into the sea with them?

Ben: She had to go back with the man to get her seal skin, and then they grew fond of each other and they had children.

Tina: Was she happy and fulfilled?

Ben: No, not really, because she was depressed and she wouldn't talk to anyone, but then, when she put her seal skin on and went back into the ocean, she was happy again.

Tina: How did she find the seal skin?

Ben: She found it in the chest the guy kept it in.

Tina: Why would the husband have kept the seal skin locked away?

Ben: Maybe he thought it was a prized possession and so she couldn't leave him.

Tina: Can you think of what this means today?

Ben: It's like a message. It's like true love.

Tina: Okay, if you're truly in love, what should you not do?

Ben: Restrict your partner from doing things. Her partner kept her from being her true self by hiding the seal skin.

Tina: Think of your own life. Is there any circumstance where you are not being true to yourself?

Ben: Well, in school I sometimes pretend I am enjoying it when I'm really not.

Tina: What has school taken away from you?

Ben: Freedom. Since school is so restrictive, I can't be creative.

Tina: If you could put on a seal skin, what would the seal skin represent for you?

Ben: If this was a physical object, it would be to do things in school that I like.

Tina: What is your seal skin? What do you do to be creative?

Ben: When I am on the computer. School is locking away technology. When I have access to technology, I feel like the character did when she found her seal skin.

Tina: Okay, let's think of another instance. Let's think about your grandfather. How is he a seal without his skin?

Ben: He was an immigrant so Canada was strange to him. He really never got his skin back, and he is kind of lost in both worlds. I know that sometimes he is still sad and misses his first home. He lost a little bit of his identity. I think that's how the seal woman felt.

Tina: How could we use the message from the story today?

Ben: You should never take anything that never belonged to you in the first place because you will probably lose it in the end anyway.

CHAPTER 4

Telling and Retelling Stories

"Tell me what your reading is about" is still the most effective way to approach students after they have read a selection, either alone or with others. We can ask them to retell the story from their own point of view. Retelling helps students activate their immediate recall of what they have heard, and each retelling will be unique. What is revealed in their retellings can give us important information about their understanding of the selection, how they internalized the content, and what they remember as significant.

Students can tell stories they have listened to and read, or participate in a variety of storytelling activities, such as these:

- relating their own anecdotes revealed by the text;
- retelling the text from a personal point of view;
- revisiting the text in role as a witness or character;
- telling other stories that connect to or grow from this text; and
- playing storytelling games and activities growing out of the text.

Before we explore how three classes used storytelling as a response mode for the selchie folktale, consider these more general ideas from master storyteller Bob Barton.

STORYTELLING — EXPLORING ITS FORMS AND POTENTIAL

Bob Barton

Storytelling includes the retelling of familiar stories as well as the development of new stories. It involves a performer narrating or enacting various roles to bring a story to life. As students retell a text, they can enrich and extend their personal hoard of words, ideas, stories, songs, and concepts, and deepen their understanding and appreciation. Storytelling develops the ability to turn narration into dialogue and dialogue into narration. Storytelling activities can take many forms.

- Students can tell stories in a circle, with a partner, in a still image or a tableau, chorally, or as narration for mime. They can improvise from the story, change the story, or find new stories to tell within the story.
- Storytelling can provide the initial starting point for drama work; it can reveal an unexplained idea in even a well-known story; it can focus particular details; it can serve as a review of what has already taken place; or it can be a way of building reflection in-role.
- Using picture books with little or no text, such as *Tuesday* by David Wiesner, students can describe in their own words what they see happening,

sometimes supplying the characters with what they believe is appropriate dialogue. Showing students unusual and exciting pictures may also promote storytelling.

- Students may enjoy playing the different characters as they tell the story. Or they may dramatize a story while it is being told, assuming the parts of different characters (e.g., a witch, a bird, or two lost students).
- As the storyteller spins the tale, you as teacher may signal for someone to continue the story, or another student may choose to take over at a dramatic pause in the story.
- In another variation, the students sit in a circle on the floor so that they can all see one another. A subject or style of story is then identified. A story is built as each student, in turn, contributes other words. A student may begin a new sentence at any appropriate moment and may add as much as he or she wishes to the story. The student who is speaking holds a talking stick, which is passed on to the next student when the speaker stops (sometimes in mid-phrase). Once the students are working easily with the activity, you may stop and start speakers at random, recognizing the threat increase for some students.
- The teacher tells an improvised story, pauses every so often, and points to someone in the group to add an appropriate word. "Once upon a time there was a young . . ." "He walked until suddenly . . ." "He said . . ."
- The teacher asks the students to imagine that they are about to go on a great adventure. The students decide individually where they are, who they are, and why they are setting forth on this adventure. Perhaps it is midnight and they are standing outside a castle, or at the edge of an enchanted forest, or in front of a modern tower block, or outside a prison camp. They must enter this place to accomplish some vital deed. They may decide that they are heroes or spies; in any case, they are to be well aware of all the attributes that such characters are likely to possess. Their journeys will be beset with dangers and difficulties.

  Now the students put their plans into action. Working individually, they begin to move off on their various quests, silently dramatizing their personal journeys. When a student feels that the quest has reached its moment of greatest tension, that student freezes.

  The students then choose partners, and each tells the other the story of his or her adventure. In the telling, the stories usually become even more exciting and the difficulties exaggerated, as do the courage and resourcefulness of the teller. Pairs may combine to make groups and small groups to make larger groups, so that eventually some students will be talking to quite a large number of others.
- The teacher chooses two narrators to share an original story between them. While the students sit in a circle, one narrator tells a short portion of the story, stops to let the other person continue, and then takes over again after a few minutes. The rest of the students become the characters and objects in the story, acting it out silently. Their participation may influence the shape of the story. This storytelling duet can also be played with the narrators providing the story and the actors making up their own speeches.
- The teacher introduces the subject of storytelling occasions, when people gather together to relate various stories. To give students practice in sustained narration, the teacher asks them to pretend that they are part of such an occasion, for example, when Robin Hood and his band of outlaws recall their

most famous escapades; when the world's greatest spies and secret agents have an annual meeting to recount their greatest exploits; or when tribe members tell stories of the deeds of their ancestors and narrate the legends of the tribe. Once the teacher has established a situation, the participants discuss their roles, and a storytelling session takes place.

Introduction to Demonstrations of Telling and Retelling Responses

In this section, you will be reminded of the power of the storyteller, where you, as teacher or invited guest, can bring tales and information to students through sharing an oral version or a read-aloud picture book about the selchie folklore.

Students, too, can engage in the art of storytelling, retelling stories they have heard, perhaps using story maps as cues for their retellings, as one class here does. You will also read about a group of student teachers who, after listening to my reading of "The Seal Wife," decided to tell their own invented stories of the selchie woman. By creating versions with different perspectives, they could share their feelings about the gender inequality of the characters; the students then retold these new versions, adding their own viewpoints. Listening to words told aloud can awaken a range of new emotionally connected responses in students.

A GUEST STORYTELLER

David Booth

I was invited to tell the story of the seal wife to a Grade 4 class in an arts-enriched alternative school in Toronto. I shared with the students Mordicai Gerstein's picture book *The Seal Mother*, reading the tale aloud and showing his illustrations. When I had finished, I asked the children for their thoughts and feelings about this folktale. Their comments revealed that they thought I was the narrator of the story and that it was my own narrative I was telling. As a guest, I was new to the class, and there had been no warm-up to the read-aloud.

EMERGENCE OF A NEW DYNAMIC

I decided to remain as the storyteller, neither confirming nor denying their conclusions. I continued my conversation with them, answering their questions, reflecting the discussion back to them as a character. The story begins with a first-person narrator saying: "Sit down, it's a long story. Accept his invitation and sit beside him. This is what he'll tell you." And then the telling of the tale of the selchie gets under way. At the conclusion of the book, the story returns to the beginning narrator's voice: "At the end of his story, the old man will pause, look at you with his deep dark eyes, and he'll wink. 'And I am one of that family,' he'll continue, 'and tonight is Midsummer's Eve.' " This line, of course, reaffirmed to the children that I was the storyteller in the book: that all this had happened to me.

Student A: I think she should have gone back to the sea.
David: She was really in a predicament, though.
Student A: Then why did she stay?
Student B: Is this story true?
David: Don't all stories hold truth within?

Student B: What do you mean?

David: Aren't all stories about truth in some way?

Student C: I agree you can find truth in stories, but did you ever see a selchie?

David: Who knows what we see or don't see in the mist, or in the swell of the waves on the sea? Who can say?

Student B: Did this happen to you?

David: I don't think that matters. It is the story I wanted you to hear. And it all happened a long, long time ago.

Student D: I know something awful about a seal. (*To teacher*) Is it appropriate if I tell everyone? (*Student whispers to teacher.*) Thanks. This is what I know. I saw a nature show on television where a great white shark attacked a grey seal and devoured it.

David: That is the rule of nature, I am afraid.

Student B: Did this happen to anyone you know?

David: The story has ended.

Would I clarify my role and my person next time? Perhaps. This time, the story became the storyteller, and a new dynamic emerged. Every sharing of a story is new; tellings continue to flourish. Guests in the classroom, and excursions, as well, bring a new context to the class, and as teachers, we have a chance to observe our students from a different point of view, which I, for one, relish.

STORY MAPS FOR RETELLING

Michelle Audoin

Michelle Audoin is a teacher with a full-day Kindergarten class at Crescent Town Public School in Toronto.

I was interested in this project because my students love stories and storytelling. I thought that it would be an opportunity for them to share the skills that they have acquired over the year and present them for an authentic purpose. Since it is Kindergarten, I knew that not all students would be interested in participating, so I left the option open to the children.

I started by reading *The Seal Mother* by Mordicai Gerstein to the entire class and sharing the pictures, taking the time to explain to them the project and their opportunity to participate, if interested. The children seemed keen. I read the book and stopped to answer questions about vocabulary and to discuss whatever they felt they needed to discuss. The children were generally interested in the fact that the father stole the selchie seal skin and that the son, Andrew, felt confused as to whether he should return the skin to his mother, or not.

The second day, I read the book to the class again, spending more time asking them probing questions about issues in the text and preparing them for the "project."

After the second reading, four students expressed interest in participating. They were given a large sheet of paper, they partnered up, and they drew story maps to help them with retelling the story. They were not given access to the book when making the story maps. They worked based on what they felt were the most important parts to tell.

I found it interesting how the book's pictures played a role in their retelling. At one point in the picture book, there is an image of the family posing for a portrait, and Andrew's mother is looking away at the seal. The children talked about this in their retellings. They also talked a lot about Andrew's dilemma about giving the skin back to his mother or not.

The children completed their story maps over two days. They were given one opportunity to rehearse and then presented their retellings, which were filmed. Their story maps helped them structure their retellings, providing a framework for them to follow.

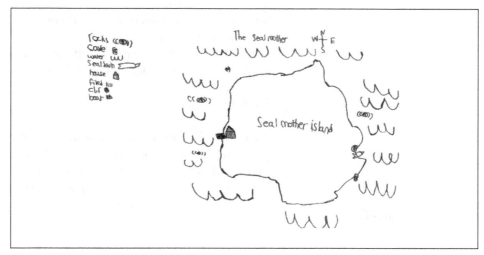

Story map of the seal mother's island

RETELLING INVENTED STORIES

David Booth

This encounter involved my working with student teachers at Wilkinson Public School in Toronto. The student teachers and I conducted a demonstration lesson together with a Grade 6 class. I wanted both student teachers and students to eventually work as storytellers.

I began by telling *The Selchie Wife*, a folktale of a Nordic seal woman, and then the student teachers, in small groups, extended the story by creating their own versions, highlighting the issues of women in that culture at that time. One group of children listened to each of the storytelling groups. After the retellings were completed, the groups of children assembled together, retold the stories of the selchie woman they had heard from the student teachers, and then added their own voices concerning the selchie's fate.

Here is how the first group began to tell the story they had heard:

Student 1: The woman as a seal was sitting on the rocks with her sisters. As the day grew longer, her sisters slipped into the water.
Student 2: She fell apart from them and was lost. At first, she was scared.
Student 3: Of humans. She had never seen them before.
Student 4: A man in a boat stole her seal skin, and now she couldn't go back to the sea. He took her back to the land.
Student 5: They watched the sunset. They were silent. She also felt love.
Student 6: He had a life with her.
Student 2: Now she had to live on the land all her life. She had two children.
Student 1: But her sister came on the land, and was trying to make a skin for her so she could go back to the sea.
David: Are you telling me that the sister is trying to bring her back to the sea?
Student 1: Yes, she had made her a skin. But then the sister who had gone to help on the land suddenly died.
Student 4: So the selchie had to decide if she should stay or go back to the sea.

David (*moving all of the class of students into role as villagers*): We as a community have to make a decision. Should we make her go back to the sea? If so, the rule is: She can never come back to the land again.

Student 3: That's not fair. She will have to see her children on the rocks by the sea once a year.

Student 2: The children will feel abandoned by their mother. They will only have a single parent.

Student 1: To see their mother on a rock in the sea is sick!

Student 4: A mother should have the right to see her children anywhere she wants.

Students: Yeah!

As we see in the transcript, student emotions ran high as they voiced their responses to the stories that were developed by the student teachers, in response to the original story. The narratives took on a life of their own, and the students struggled to make sense of complex issues drawn from folklore but constructed and told by the student teachers.

CHAPTER 5

Reading and Viewing Connected Texts

As we support our students in their development as readers of different text forms, we need to consider how we can help them to strategically read the texts from home and school, whether it will be a manga novel or a poetry anthology, on a hand-held electronic reader or on a computer screen.

By focusing on and teaching about different collections of connected texts, sometimes called *text sets*, we can help students look at reading and writing experiences in different ways, increasing the breadth of their literacy experiences and deepening their understanding of the function of particular texts. For example, this book has incorporated several versions of the selchie tales, and some classes explored different texts. Teachers and school librarians often work together to build groups of connected texts, including information books and online sites about the content's themes and issues, as well as films, pictures, and songs. Students themselves can locate similar texts from public or school libraries or from online sites.

Comparing and Using Related Texts

We can encourage students to select texts of different types and to bring in resources that they think complement the original text. We can discuss with the students characteristics, or rules, of the text, comparing these characteristics with other texts, and charting similarities and differences. Students can engage in the following related activities:

- reading other texts, in print and online, connected to the theme, concept, style, or culture of the original;
- locating background information and research by reading about the author or illustrator from websites;
- reading nonfiction texts that relate to the original;
- finding reviews and reports about the book, the time, the setting, or the author;
- reading related texts written by other students;
- interviewing guest authors and illustrators who visit;
- creating book talks on a theme or concept that the author explores;
- attending a young authors' conference;
- reading about authors, their views, and their lives on their websites;
- writing and publishing books they have written; and
- setting up special text celebrations for the whole school.

We can also organize writing projects in which students are engaged in constructing their ideas within the genre.

Considering ways to classify stories

As teachers, we can help the students classify or categorize stories by theme, type, or story attributes. Consider the options that were incorporated in this book project on selchie tales:

- Variations of the same folktale motif:
  The Seal Mother by Mordicai Gerstein and *Seal Song* by Andrea Spalding
- Cultural variants of the same tale:
  The Boy Who Lived with the Seals (An Aboriginal Tale) by Rafe Martin
- Different versions of the same story:
  The Selchie Girl by Susan Cooper and *Greyling* by Jane Yolen
- Same story pictured by different illustrators:
  The Seal Song, illustrated by Pascal Milelli and *The Boy Who Lived with the Seals*, illustrated by David Shannon
- Stories with similar structures:
  Una and the Sea Cloak by Malachy Doyle
- Stories on a particular theme or topic:
  Neptune Rising by Jane Yolen
- Texts of specific genres:
  Poems of Magic and Spells, edited by William Cole
- Books by one author or illustrator:
  Neptune Rising and *Here There Be Unicorns* by Jane Yolen
- Stories with the same characters:
  The Selchie Girl by Susan Cooper and *Greyling* by Jane Yolen
- Stories from the same culture:
  The Norse Myths by Kevin Crossley-Holland
- Stories with similar motifs:
  The Crane Wife by Katherine Paterson

Our involvement with connected texts takes many forms. We ask questions about one text and look for answers in another; we search for a sequel or a prequel; we find another book by the author; we view a film version of the book; we read several reviews to compare our own opinions; we listen to songs or singers, connected to the text; we choose a passage from the text and copy it for a friend. We make connections to the texts that are broadening our understanding — we continue to learn.

Questions to Prompt Reflection on Use of Text Sets

- How will we as teachers build extensive text sets that change students' perceptions and points of view, cause wider connections to open up, and promote conceptual understanding?
- How will we weave together the texts from the Internet with the texts from the library, from magazines, from interviews?
- How will we expand our students' construct of the world through the texts they encounter in and outside our classes?
- Can we connect other writings to the text we are focusing on? (Perhaps a series, a sequel, an autobiography, a picture book, online information.)
- Can we gently nudge the students into finding patterns in the things the author writes about, in the events of the stories, in the characters, in the ideas the author seems to believe in, and in the style of the writing?

- Have we found, or directed the students towards, any information about the author or incorporated a YouTube video of the author speaking?
- How will we connect the texts of the classroom to the texts of our students' lives?

As we share one text with students, they can make connections to others with similar themes or issues, characters, or settings.

Introduction to Demonstrations of Responding to Connected Texts

Three innovative demonstrations of how teachers have addressed the selchie folk-tale through this response mode follow. We found several tellings of the selchie tales, and I was able to read different versions, with some classes focusing on a particular one. In this section, you will meet students who responded to a book with a similar plot involving a mermaid and another class that asked questions about a very different version. Comparison is an immediate opening to discussion and can lead to significant interpretive and critical thinking. Stories lead to other stories.

STORY PATTERNS: DEEPENING STORY KNOWLEDGE

Gillian Wortley

In this article, Gillian Wortley describes response activities undertaken by her students in Grades 1 and 2 at da Vinci School, Toronto.

Una and the Sea Cloak is a magical story that has many compelling features that appeal to young children: fantastical flying creatures that can also swim under the sea, mermaids, the interface of human and magic, themes of a quest, rescue, and redemption. The book has magnificent illustrations and endless possibilities for drama, dance, and artistic extension. I chose it for these reasons and because it has been a favorite story in our own family. My husband and I have shared it with our own three daughters, over and over and over again, and each time, my husband, the girls, and I find something new to wonder about, notice, or reflect on, either in the text or in the illustrations.

My students and I explored *Una and the Sea Cloak* by Malachy Doyle and *The Seal Mother* by Mordicai Gerstein, over four lessons.

LESSON 1: OF VENN DIAGRAMS AND MAGICAL CLOAKS

Comparing story versions: After hearing both stories, the Grades 1 and 2 students worked in small groups to build a Venn diagram about the similarities and differences between the two versions. The diagram below is a compilation of their points.

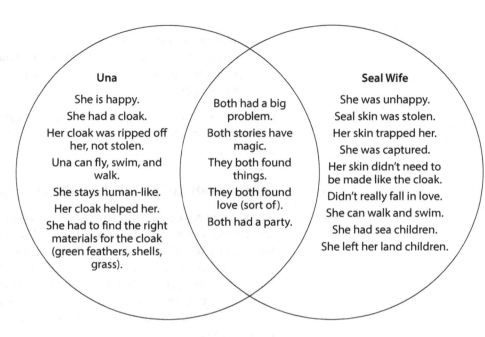

Una

She is happy.

She had a cloak.

Her cloak was ripped off her, not stolen.

Una can fly, swim, and walk.

She stays human-like.

Her cloak helped her.

She had to find the right materials for the cloak (green feathers, shells, grass).

Both had a big problem.

Both stories have magic.

They both found things.

They both found love (sort of).

Both had a party.

Seal Wife

She was unhappy.

Seal skin was stolen.

Her skin trapped her.

She was captured.

Her skin didn't need to be made like the cloak.

Didn't really fall in love.

She can walk and swim.

She had sea children.

She left her land children.

A graphic organizer showing similarities and differences between Una and the Seal Wife

Flying and diving into the story: Before sharing the story with the children, I did a short introductory drama with them. I gave them all a cloak to hold in their arms (imaginary, of course). I asked them to examine the cloak in their arms, to notice the soft silky green threads that appeared to be silken grasses, the shimmery shells, and the strange and wonderful green feathers.

"Where could these materials be from?" I asked. I prompted the children to try the cloak on. "How does it feel? What does it weigh? Is it light or heavy?"

I then told them that this was a cloak with magical powers. When they wore this cloak, they could fly in the sky. I invited them to experiment with flying while wearing the cloak. "Up beyond the trees, past white fluffy clouds, amongst flocks of birds in flight, feel the wind through your hair, feel your cloak fluttering behind you. Try flying higher, feeling the warmth of the sun . . ."

I then asked them to see whether they could dive into the water. "Now try diving down towards the sea." Their sea cloak let them breathe under water and be part of the underwater world. "Swim past schools of fish, forests of beautiful, colorful coral. Dive past sharks and whales, swim with pods of dolphins, and frolic in the warm waves.

"Now swim to a nearby ocean and walk out to the beach. Wander down the soft sandy beach and look for shells, wearing your shimmery, magical sea cloak.

"Climb the rocky cliff on the edge of the beach and once you reach the top, launch yourself off to fly in the sky again. As you are flying, you notice a band of dark storm clouds in the distance. These clouds are coming closer and closer, they begin to surround you, to toss you in their wild winds and throw you wildly and uncontrollably around and around. You are caught in a terrible storm. The winds take you and pull you down, down, down, crashing you on the beach. Your cloak is torn and you are exhausted. You lie there until you fall asleep, cold and afraid."

On the beach and on the page: The children were then invited to the carpet for the read-aloud. I showed them the book and asked them to activate their schema and tell me about any other books they had read about the sea or about creatures from the sea. Had they heard of mermaids or any tales of mermaids? They had many stories and connections they wanted to discuss, for example, stories of mermaids swimming up to ships and of humans having a chance to meet them. They even had stories of magical mermaids causing humans to fall into danger.

I then shared the story until Una is caught in the storm and thrown on the beach — they could scarcely bear the thought of waiting another day to finish it! The students were invited to write in their Reading Response books either from the perspective of Una, caught in the storm, or from Martin, who finds the girl on the beach.

LESSON 2: ROLE-PLAYING POSSIBILITIES

The next lesson began with predictions based on their schema or their imaginations. I encouraged them to think of possibilities and directions the story could go in. We read up until the moment when Una is brought into Martin's house and put to bed to rest.

The children were then put into groups of three so that they could act out the scene where Martin and his mother urge Una to tell them what her cloak is made of in order for the mother to repair it. Each character playing Martin went on a quest to find the grasses while the mothers stayed home to nurse the ill and weak Una.

The students were invited to return to the carpet to hear more of the story, up to the point when Martin returns home with the grasses. They then returned to their Reading Response books to write in role as their character. They added a picture each time they completed their writing.

LESSON 3: LAUNCHING INTO DANCE

The children were welcomed to the carpet for the day's read-aloud. They were then asked to recall what had happened and to predict what could happen. Doing this helped them understand the developing structure of the story and identify ways that the story could play out. Each day I asked them to use their schema to tell me if they could make any connections to any other story they had read or film they had seen. We read until the end of the story.

Reflecting on a wonderful idea: We then reflected on the end of the story. They were so excited by the banquet where the humans were magically able to travel under the sea to visit Una's parents so that they could thank them for saving Una. For these children, it was the most wonderful idea to think it could be possible to have access to a magical underwater kingdom by donning a cloak.

Dancing story meaning: I told them that we were going to experience the story in dance. Before doing so we discussed the particularly evocative vocabulary that might help them express the meaning of the story in movement. We discussed the word *launch* as this is what Una does to come into flight. With our bodies we experimented with what it might feel like to launch off a cliff to fly.

We discussed the elements of dance (body, energy, space, and timing) and how to incorporate these into their creative movement to convey meaning and expression. I asked them to work together and then played a song, "Earth Song" by Michael Jackson, a piece that grows and develops in intensity, throughout the lesson.

The children shared their dance/movement creations with the class. They did some extremely beautiful work, and all the children were enthusiastic.

LESSON 4: WEAVING WORDS AND WOOLS

Reflection: Children were asked to share, on the carpet, their favorite parts of the story and to discuss what they felt was most moving. I encouraged them to write one more piece, either about their flight with Una or Martin and his mother or about the banquet.

A hand-made cloak: The final piece connected to this story was for the class to weave Una's sea cloak. I had prepared a cardboard weaving frame and some beautiful weaving wools. The wools are very soft, some of it green roving (unspun strands of fibre), looking and feeling magical, almost like sea grass. I also had some shells with holes drilled into them (thanks to parents) and some green feathers. Children took turns weaving the cloak until it was finished.

PROVIDING MULTIPLE WAYS TO RESPOND

When I ask my students to respond to text, I know I can deepen their level of understanding and their relationship to it by providing multiple ways for them to respond beyond simple paper and pencil. I allow them to talk and listen to each other while they make connections orally. I also prompt them to draw what affects them deeply, using high-quality art materials, such as beeswax crayons and pencil crayons with beautiful pigments. We experience text through drama and sometimes by movement, bringing to life the experiences read in the text, exploring the emotions and problems encountered by the characters. Can students come up with ways of moving forward through these problems, contributing to the story, extending it, replaying and re-creating it? They think themselves in and out through the text. They can experience and respond to it on many levels — cognitively, physically, and emotionally, even tactile, in the case of the sea cloak weaving. I would hear them talking about how silky their fingers felt weaving the sea grasses.

Here's how one child, Isabel, responded to her work on the story: "I loved dancing how I felt, swimming and walking with my repaired sea cloak."

The children wove the cloak, strand by strand.

Gillian Wortley puts her experiences with the four lessons outlined above into a more general context of children making use of their imaginations.

MAPPING OUR COMPREHENSION

Laura Hughes

Teacher Laura Hughes describes working with her Grade 1 students at Crescent Town Public School in Toronto.

Day One: On the first day we talked about what background knowledge the children had in terms of ocean life. We drew on our study of living things and discussed seals and other creatures of the North. We looked at maps and talked about the weather and the landscape. Then we looked at the cover of *The Seal Mother* and made simple predictions about what might happen in the story. Together, we created a chart of questions. Who is the Seal Mother, I wonder . . .

Day Two: We began our read-aloud of the story. When we got to the part where Andrew hears his name being called, we closed the book and made predictions about what Andrew would choose to do when he leaned into the cave and found the seal skin. Would he give it to his mother? Would he hide it so his mother wouldn't leave? Would he tell his mother and let her decide what she wanted to do? The children did a Think-Pair-Share activity, where they sat with a partner and shared their ideas, then, if they felt comfortable, presented to the group. Using stickers, we created a graph to tally our predictions. Most children sympathized with the mother and felt Andrew would give the skin to her without question.

Day Three: When the children came to class they found a large picture of Andrew on the easel. I asked them to think back to the day before and the difficult decision Andrew needed to make. In the center of the classroom, I placed a small square carpet. I explained to the children that when they stepped onto the mat, they would instantly become Andrew. I invited them to think out loud as Andrew dealt with his difficult choice, and I videotaped several of these performances — they were inspiring. Then each child was given a paper cut in the shape of a speech bubble and asked to imagine himself or herself as Andrew. What would they say if they were to think out loud? We placed the speech bubbles all around the drawing of Andrew.

Students wrote on speech bubbles in role as Andrew.

Day Four: We read the rest of the story and reflected on Andrew's physical journey. Where did he start out, and where did he end up? Where did his mother come from, and where did she go? Where was the seal skin hidden, and where did Andrew live? We brainstormed a list of physical places in the story and then, based on our knowledge of the Grade 1 mapping curriculum, we each drew maps. Every map was unique. Some had a compass rose; others had landforms and features from students' imaginations. Beautiful results!

Day Five: We returned to the sea and the passage in the story about the magical underwater world of sea cows and crystal palaces. I asked the children to imagine and create an oil pastel drawing of the underwater world. We then painted with watercolor to create a resist and sprinkled with salt to make the texture of bubbles and flowing water.

This was my first experience with the text, and I was encouraged to see the many rich learning opportunities that the children could find within the one story. I let the children's interests guide me along, and they were genuinely eager to continue with the story for the full week. I was amazed by the deep emotions each child conveyed and by their ability to express themselves in role.

"There's the shark, he is swimming. The crab is eating water. The fish is eating his food. The seal mother is there."
(Jobaer)

One student's image of the selchie's underwater world

DRUMMING A HEARTBEAT

Sarah Craig

Normally, students in my Grade 2 class respond to stories in the usual ways: through discussion, writing, art, or drama; however, for the story *Greyling*, a presentation given by a drumming club from a local Barrie, Ontario, school inspired a different type of story response.

I decided we would examine Greyling's heartbeat at four points in the story and, using a drum, try to represent how it might sound. The points we would focus on were as follows: (1) when he was stranded on the sand bar as a pup; (2) when he stood by the shore, grieving as he looked out to sea; (3) when he exclaimed heroically to his mother that he would save his drowning father; and (4) when he shed his human skin and became a seal once again.

We began with a read-aloud, stopping at each of the four points to discuss Greyling's emotional state, why he would be feeling that way, and whether the children had ever felt that way. I asked the students to pretend to be Greyling at each point and to show how they thought his heart would be beating by moving their hands over their own hearts. I then had them draw that beating heart with a heartbeat line. Finally, we went to the drums. Each child experimented to find a drumbeat that would represent the sound of the heartbeats he or she had drawn. I asked the students to find some way of recording this, so that they could play it back later for the group.

When all the heartbeats had been recorded, we began the drumming. I acted as the conductor, holding up one through four fingers to indicate the different heartbeats as they drummed. We drummed around the circle, hearing each child's interpretation of Greyling's feelings. All of the children had different ways of interpreting and drumming Greyling's heartbeat at each of the four points of the story.

Afterwards, the children suggested other situations where our hearts might beat in a particular way, and we tried these heartbeats out on the drums:

- when you are falling asleep (Nate);
- how it would feel when you're about to trip but you don't (Waseem);
- when you are dying (Devlyn);
- when I go back to Dad's and won't see Mom for a long time (Avah); and
- when you get a goal in basketball (Mandela).

A NOVEL AND POWERFUL WAY OF RESPONDING

Experiencing the emotions of another by feeling Greyling's heartbeat was a novel way for my students to respond to a story. Students who are not strong writers and those who have trouble articulating their ideas orally were able to express themselves successfully with this non-verbal type of response. We had a lot of fun — it is very satisfying to make noise with a drum. A heartbeat is an elemental sound we all understand and can re-create easily without any percussion expertise.

The children had the strongest connection to the part of the story where the seal pup was crying for its family on the sand bar. They understood this heartbeat best (see the diagram on the next page); all of them had had an experience of being separated from their parents and knew how scared and lonely Greyling would have felt. Alana said: "I was stranded in a store once, and I was very scared. That drumming felt like a real heartbeat."

Drumming provided a way for my students to understand a story character, and through that character, something of themselves. It has now become another tool in my story-response toolkit.

			Name: Arah
Greyling			
[it was] stranded on the sand bar, crying for its own.	...he often stood by the shore or high in the town on the great grey cliffs, looking and longing and grieving his in his heart for what he did not really know...	"I will save him, Mother, or die as I try."	And as Greyling went deeper beneath the waves, even his skin seemed to slough off till he swam, free at last, in the sleek grey coat of a great grey seal.
(Draw Greyling's heartbeat as he might feel it at each of these stages of the story.)			
(Now represent Greyling's heartbeat through drumming. Use words or symbols to record how you will play the drum to show his different emotional states.) a Quiet steddy beat 2 hands	Such a Quiet heart beat you can barelay here it 3 you go smooth 1 hand	it's starting to sound mediam 2 hands	Verry verry verry verry verry verry verry verry fast 2 hands

The children each created a chart, as in an electrocardiogram, to represent the different heart rhythms that the selchie Greyling would have experienced in different situations.

CHAPTER 6

Giving Voice to Words in Print

Students benefit from opportunities to give voice to words they have previously read. That is what they are doing when they discuss a book with the teacher, report on information they have researched, introduce a guest speaker, or read a group of poems aloud. The audience receives their message live but understands that there has been premeditation. Students can find effective reasons for engaging in these activities, all founded on print:

- reading aloud,
- giving book talks,
- making presentations,
- reporting on Internet findings,
- participating in debates,
- making reports,
- giving speeches,
- performing in play presentations,
- giving and conducting interviews,
- making announcements,
- sharing their writing, and
- reading to younger students.

The Value of Oral Reading

Students find that reading aloud lets them share their understanding of the text and experiment with new language styles, voices, and patterns of speaking. Oral reading verifies print and helps silent readers to "hear" dialogue. Small groups can come together for oral reading, or older students can read stories they have prepared for younger listeners, or the class can join together in the choral reading of a poem. Oral interpretation, when done well, can improve all the skills of comprehension, lead to revelation for the readers themselves, and strengthen how readers understand both the text and themselves as readers; it offers opportunities for finding and sharing voice while inside the printed words.

Exploring and sharing the text

Students need opportunities to explore a text before reading it aloud. If they do *not* first examine the text, "rub up against it," notice how others are feeling and wondering, question private belief, expand information, and hear the voices of print struggling for freedom, they will be sharing print aloud for no effective reason. Sometimes, it is the reader who is listening best, learning through ear and eye at the same time.

- *Music making.* My colleague Lee Willingham brings music to our faculty of education as he engages our student teachers in all kinds of music making and learning — which, by definition, includes oral reading. He writes:

  > There is nothing quite like the buzz you experience when your expressive voice, full of energy and resolve, *sings* a profoundly personal emotion from deep within. The act of music making that is engaged in the human spirit far surpasses the knowledge that one has in reading notation or mastering the theory, or the skill that one may have acquired in being able to reproduce a pitch exactly in tune. It is musical understanding.

- *Readers theatre.* This technique allows the students to dramatize narration or selections from novels, short stories, folklore, picture books, or poems, instead of reading aloud only scripted material. The students can have one person read the narration while others read the dialogue speeches, or they can explore who could read the different lines. For example, a character who speaks dialogue may also read the information in the narration that refers to him or her. Several students can read narration as a chorus. Little body movement is used in Readers theatre; instead, emphasis is placed on vocal performance.

- *Highlights for sharing.* At the conclusion of a particular theme or unit, students can read interesting or significant findings, poems that touched them, excerpts that made connections, quotations from novels, or personal writings from journals or writing folders that they feel will have special appeal for their class.

- *Presentation of ideas and work.* We can use the curriculum to create low-threat learning contexts that encourage sharing work-in-progress and presenting completed ideas and information. When students share ideas first with partners or small groups rather than with the whole class, they can develop into confident speakers with something to say. Letting students use notes and various aids, such as PowerPoint or chalkboard diagrams, can support their efforts at formal presentations.

The Ritual of Sharing

The ritual of sharing and summarizing is vital to oral reading in many aspects of community life. We can incorporate this power of oral response into classroom teaching.

Introduction to Demonstrations of Giving Voice to Printed Words

As the selchie stories and poems are read aloud by the students, they come to grips with the whole meaning-making world of oral interpretation. How will the words of a poem be spoken, so that the original tale will be understood? How will students determine for themselves what characters mean when they speak in print? Who will the narrator be? In what style will the story be told — documentary, humorous, mystery? How will we learn to read those new or difficult words? How will we build in enough rehearsal so the words of the tale told in poetry will be honored? Such are the questions that can be explored when students read aloud for real reasons. The three articles that follow outline demonstrations of effective use of the response mode referred to as "giving voice to words in print" in this resource. The students first explore the ideas in the text and then make several attempts at reading the words out loud until they are secure in their own interpretations. Oral reading requires experimenting with how words sound and mean. We can let the words sing.

FROM WORDS THAT *MEAN* TO WORDS THAT *SPEAK*

Amah Harris

Amah Harris teaches a Grade 7 regular program integrated with Special Education students in Toronto.

The experience of the poem "Ballad of the White Seal Maid" [see the Appendix] came to my Grade 7 class the final month of the school year. June saw them deeply involved in completing major projects for their final term. At that stage, they had already lived the experience of drama as pedagogy framed in socio-cultural theory, synergized with an emergent pedagogy, where the child is central to, rather than included in, the learning process.

Here, it is important to note that the month of May had seen the culmination of their *choreo-poetry* dramas. Given that they had had that experience, how would I introduce this experience to them to excavate the gems of learning embedded in the text? Their imaginations would need to be the tool — making connections is a key to unlock the imagination. I decided to have them explore the poem in three stages. I began with the whole-class analysis.

1. EMERGENCE OF A DIALOGIC PROCESS

We sat in a circle, each student with a copy of the text. They delved into the text in silence, save one who needed to read aloud the poem to himself. I simply asked them to read and then share their thoughts. After 10 to 15 minutes, hands began to shoot into the air, and students stood and shared their ideas.

Several began with a literal interpretation; three, however, had already begun to excavate. All three hooked onto the phrase "A rock, a rock in his heart." Interestingly enough, all three gave completely different interpretations. This entry excavation proved a feeding ground for a dialogic process beyond dialogue, as each response grew from what was heard and built on it, digging deeper and deeper into the heart of the text. There was quite an intensity of discussion. I did not direct the discussion; rather, I allowed the students' own responses to direct it. They challenged each other's ideas, agreed, then challenged again, and so the discussion took on its own life. At this point, they seemed ready for the next stage: choral dramatization of the piece.

2. INTERPRETATION THROUGH CHORAL DRAMATIZATION

The students decided that they wanted to choose their own teams. What excitement, even tears, when some members of one group got caught up in friendship rather than in interpretation! Always a possibility when one chooses friends. There was intervention, disagreements were settled, and dramatization of the piece developed. In another group, one student of European descent decided to become the selchie maid's skin over the body of a student of African descent. How graphic it became when that skin was shed! What depth of meaning to be read into that interpretation! What happens when that skin is put back on . . .?

The choral readers in each group took turns bringing to light their insight into the text as the dramatization of the poem unfolded. The students were enthralled with the work of their classmates. They clapped and commented on each sharing, sometimes giving their own interpretation of the reading experienced.

ON THE SPOT IN ROLE

Here, an unexpected infusion fed beautifully into the final stage. Professor Booth took leadership. He asked the boys to stand. His questions placed them in role as the fisherman with the villagers knowing that they had forcibly kept the selchie's skin from her. Most responded emphatically that they were not ashamed of what they had done. Even the male student who, throughout the year, criticized both students and teachers on any comments that seemed to approach sexism or any of the other isms, felt that way. In fact, he was the first to respond. They all used the fisherman's lonely, sad situation to justify what he had done. After such serious analysis and dramatic presentations, a few even laughed while responding. The boys voiced the opinion that the selchie would forgive them eventually.

Then it was the girls' turn. Some shouted their responses. They called the fisherman abusive and inhumane. They said that he had stolen their freedom and was guilty of sexism, slavery, and cruel behavior. When asked whether they would forgive the fisherman, they were unanimous in their answer: No!

3. DEEP REVIEW

The final stage occurred the next day, the last day of school after the class had played competitive sports with the other Grade 7 students. The students were asked to bring in their copies of the poem, find a private space, reread the poem, and write comments on it, keeping in mind whether the fisherman should be forgiven or not. The students got back to the poem as if they had never left it. It seemed to have touched a chord in all of them, as demonstrated by their commitment. They were told they had 40 minutes to write their comments; some asked for and received more time.

Their excavations had deepened, their analysis becoming even more insightful. The girls, on different levels, gave an analysis of the poem that supported their decision not to forgive the fisherman for what they saw as generally sexist and abusive behavior. The boys were divided. Most felt ashamed for what the fisherman had done, also calling his behavior sexist and abusive; they said he should not have behaved as he did. A few were more empathetic, trying to understand why the fisherman would have behaved in that manner. Instead of calling his behavior sexist or abusive, these boys said that after seeing how the selchie maid responded to the fisherman stealing her skin, they regretted that he had behaved as he did; they did not feel that the behavior was worth it in the end.

REFLECTIONS FROM THE BOYS SPEAKING AS THE FISHERMAN

The comments below pertain to both the choral dramatization and the class discussion. They provide a cross-section of opinion.

"The fisherman was lonely so he was desperate to find a girl," said Jordan. "It was wrong to just steal her but if I was lonely I would do the same thing, but ask her. I could tell that in the story the fisherman had 'A rock, a rock in his heart,' which to me means he had a cold and big lump in his heart because he was sad. I think the author meant taking away your skin is like taking away your freedom. I know this because men/women go to jail and their skin/freedom is gone."

Taylor had this to say: "Well I think 'a rock, a rock in his heart' means he seems to be always feeling blue and blue is a very cool sad colour, so to me it is a great word to describe him and when he took the selchie maid's seal skin he forced love on her and he said now you must come with me and he was just taking claim to a wife. That is just awful. If I was her I would never forgive him because I would never trust him again. How could I live with someone so mean?"

As for Abdul, he said: "My first impression was that I felt bad for the fisherman because he was lonely and depressed, but after the mermaid came he took

An Interesting Aside

Later in the day, as the class was playing a year's sum-up game not connected to the selchie poem, one male student turned to a young girl with whom he felt quite close, and said " . . . would you have forgiven, Tina?" The girl paused, as if sensing his need for forgiveness. She responded quietly, "Yes, I would've." The game continued.

her skin and said, 'you are coming with me now' which sounded abusive. Taking her skin was also abusive. Then I thought the fisherman was abusive instead of a lonely, depressed man. I for sure would not have forgiven that man because being abusive to women is really bad, and men and women should have the same rights. Being abusive to a woman doesn't make you any stronger or more powerful; it just makes people more scared and they won't want to be with you."

One male student, Steve, gave this in-role response: "Yes, I do regret stealing the girl's skin because I loved her and wanted her so bad but now that she's gone and hates me, I've realized it wasn't worth it. The skin represents her heart, and taking it is like killing the person, denying them power because once your heart dies you as the person die. You shut down and can't live anymore. She is under his control now her freedom was taken from her."

Finally, one student offered this assessment: "I think our class underestimated the story. They thought it was about love but later found out how cruel the fisherman is. He took a woman's livelihood and kept her trapped. That sounds more like abuse than love. If I was the fisherman, I would never do that because violence is against human rights. If I were the woman/maid, I would have really killed the man for what he has done. The skin was a part of the woman's life but the fisherman took it, which is just cruel. Even from the beginning, the fisherman had no heart ('a rock, a rock in his heart'). He never took the time to think how the woman felt. The skin is like the fisherman's boat: without it, he is dead inside, just like the skin is to the maid."

HOW CREATING BACKSTORIES STRENGTHENS STUDENTS' ORAL READING

David Booth with Grant Minkhorst

I had the pleasure of working with Grant Minkhorst and his Grade 7 students in a school in Oakville during this project. Because I had worked before with Grant and his students, I selected a quite difficult version of the story, *Kopakona — The Seal Woman*, a lengthy poem by Anne Born, from Nordic and Danish origins, in which the story is told as a monologue by the fisherman who originally had found the seal skin. In this telling, the poet moves us into the world of the seal hunters, and the climax involves the death of the seal woman. (The ballad "The Great Silkie of Sule Skerry" tells a similar tale and can be found online at www.sacred-texts.com.)

I read the students the poem aloud as they followed along from copies, and then volunteers retold the tale, adding information in sequence as they remembered it. The images painted by the poet, delivered by the fisherman, are dark, and the syntax was unfamiliar in places for the students, as in these lines below:

Down by the shore, a low form, then another,
  Out of the sea
They came, a group of ten or twelve, closer.

Students were divided into groups, with each group responsible for one verse. As part of rehearsal, all the groups read their sections aloud at the same time, helping each other with unknown or unusual words and phrases, clarifying where the lines should stop and how pauses should work. I tried to answer their unsolved queries, and we read the poem aloud again, with members of each group responsible for reading a line or two.

CREATING A BACKSTORY FOR A LISTENING CHARACTER

The students had further questions, so as a class, we discussed how the lines might be divided for speakers so they would have greater impact, how punctuation might help with fluency, and who the listeners might be.

We read the poem aloud again, and as they listened to other students reading their lines, the students began to understand who might be listening. I left them with an assignment, to be completed by my return visit in a couple of weeks. They were to each select a character who could be listening to the poem and to create *a backstory* for that character, so in future, as they read the poem, they could envisage the people who would have been affected by this tragic episode.

Their teacher, Grant, continued exploring the poem and the backstories with them, and worked with them developing their roles, their characters. The students began to write down in monologue form their observations and recollections of what had happened, taking on the voices of other fishermen who hunted seals, of relatives of the seal woman — her children (both on land and in the sea), her grandmother who now had to raise the children abandoned by their mother, a marine biologist, a twin brother of the husband, and many more.

By the time I returned to the class, their stories had been revised several times, edited, and formatted on a computer. There were also pencil sketches of their characters.

CRAFTED RESPONSES TO ORAL TELLINGS

For suggestions on how to promote authentic oral reading events in the classroom, see *This Book Is Not about Drama*, a resource I co-authored with Myra Barrs and Bob Barton. The book offers sources and suggestions for helping students bring to life printed texts, including poems, scripts, stories, and information, so that they come to understand what they are reading aloud and extend their ability to interpret that text with meaning.

The class presented the bound copy to me, and then I asked them to once again read aloud the poem. I arranged them in different groups, with some group members sitting and some standing. Some had memorized their lines, and all spoke them with strong, confident voices. Grant's teaching and mentoring rang out clearly, and later, I interviewed several students in role as the character they had chosen. Their monologues were filled with the truths of the tale, interpreted with the authentic voice and disposition of the speaker. The stories were crafted responses to the oral telling of the poem, and the words of the poem read aloud were performed with nuanced delivery.

Reading text aloud can be a powerful tool for literacy, and if the students explore the context for the words — the content of the text — and construct a frame to hold the oral telling, then they will better understand how words are read aloud and how the voice of the reader creates meaning for the listeners. Grant supports his students into discovering new-found strengths as readers, writers, and speakers. It is always a pleasure to see his students in action.

CASSIOPEIA, KOPAKONA'S FRIEND ON LAND

. . . Even though it was expected, Cassiopeia still couldn't get over that Kopakona left her behind. Cassiopeia is an orphan, she still is, but in the past Kopakona was there to cheer her up. Now 16, Cassiopeia finally accepted it, right when she accept it, new rumors started. It seemed like Kopakona was a selkie, and that she had been imprisoned by her own husband. Although it was a prison without chains, a prison it still is. I also heard that selkies need their seal skins to go back to the ocean, and that her husband hid her seal skin from her. And when Kopakona finally found a way back to where she belongs — the ocean — she was caught and slaughtered. And it was all her husband's fault, for he kept her on land, away from her home. Even in death, she was caught in the devil's hand . . .

Catherine

KOPAKONA'S ELDEST HUMAN SON

. . . I found out how my mother died on my 13th birthday. My father told me how my mother was killed. I was in shock to find my own mother was murderd, my father told me that she was half seal, half human. I thought my dad had lost a few pieces to the puzzle, then he brought me to the cave that he found her seal skin at the time of year all the seal people gathered to dance. They were mo[u]rning for the seals who died in the massacre. I started to well up because I knew what they were feeling, the shock and the pain of knowing that they would never see them again.

KOPAKONA'S HUSBAND, OLAF THE VIKING

. . . In sorrow, after the death of his precious wife. It became worse with the Seabird's howls, winds, and waves accusing him for her death. He could have dealt with this horrible situation more suitable without accusations. now Olaf has his seven children to raise on his own, he is lost, and broken down. Feeling regretful since the Twelfth night.

Taevanh

Student illustration accompanying writing in role from perspective of the selchie's eldest human son

THE SELCHIE STORY AS READERS THEATRE

Shelley Murphy

Shelley Murphy is an instructor at the Ontario Institute for Studies in Education, University of Toronto.

A group of fifth graders sits around a table exchanging suggestions, interpretations, feedback, and laughter as they negotiate their separate and shared meaning-making of a text. They have been preparing and rehearsing their Readers theatre script of a poem called *The Seal Child* for the past week. The four students will soon happily upload a digital recording of their interpretive reading of the poem to the class website *and* perform it live for the enjoyment of others. Only months before this same group of students viewed reading, silent or otherwise, as something to be avoided at all costs. That they would come to view reading as a creative, meaningful, and enjoyable experience had never occurred to them. It was Readers theatre that provided the entry point for this discovery.

Readers theatre is an interpretive activity in which readers bring characters, story, poetry, and even content-area material to life through their voices. Students read from a script that is not memorized. Unlike drama, in which body movement reveals a great deal of meaning, Readers theatre is dependent on the quality of the readers' voices to capture the listener. Student performers, through their voices, interpret and convey the emotions, beliefs, attitudes, and motives of

"Words mean more than what is set down on paper. It takes the human voice to infuse them with deeper meaning."
— Maya Angelou

the literary characters for the audience. In order for students to do so, they must come to a deep understanding of the story and its characters.

Although Readers theatre is intended to be shared with an audience, it is a process-oriented activity. This powerful process takes place in a small-group setting where students cooperate with each other to negotiate, refine, and practice their interpretations of text. It is during this interactive, cooperative work that the power of Readers theatre as a literacy-building strategy emerges. I have found fewer better strategies for building fluency and stronger and more motivated readers, and for deepening students' connections to text.

Take our group of fifth graders. After a few rounds of Readers theatre experiences, they were given the poem *The Seal Child* to prepare for a Readers theatre presentation the following week. Their initial instructions were to read the poem silently and to jot notes about their thoughts, ideas, and interpretations of the different lines in the poem and the poem in its entirety. Students were reminded that there were no wrong answers as poems, in particular, are often written in a way that invites readers to figure out and interpret their meaning for themselves.

I also asked our students to think about how their voices could be used as instruments to support the meaning of the poem, as in *Poetry: Powerful Thoughts in Tiny Packages*, where students are told that poems are like music and they must listen for the song a poem is trying to sing. With this in mind, students used sticky notes to record ideas to help guide them in their search for the music in their poem, namely, where to have breaks, where to emphasize certain words, where to slow down, where to speak louder or softer, and so on, to convey certain meanings.

After spending 15 minutes or so with their poems individually, our four fifth graders came together as a group to discuss and share their meaning making and their ideas about conveying this meaning through their Readers theatre presentations. Each of them had read and reread the poem several times and had now come to the group with some notes to share. They each took their turn.

Miguel: I think *The Seal Child* is a little sad because it's about someone who lives with his mom for half the time and his father for the other half and it's so different. That must be really hard. I know some kids who have to do that.

Vincent: Yeah, but he gets to live in the land and the sea. But, I think he's happier in the sea. When he saw his dad he ran to him. He must be happier in the sea. I think when we read the lines "my home is free inside the sea" it should be happy like this . . .

Vincent reads the line with a tone and verve that convey joy.

Britney: That sounds good. But in the second last stanza it says, "his time is shared, his love for both has been declared." I think the boy has learned to live in both and to love both equally. I think it's the dad that's happier in the sea. He's the one that would sound really happy when he's saying, "my home is free inside the sea." What do you think?

The rest of the group members turn their pages to the second last stanza and read.

Vincent: You know what? I think you're right.

Nadia: And I think the Seal Child got used to both and it's the dad that likes the sea more. I think he comes onto land just to get his son. For our Readers theatre we could read the first part, "I am a man upon the land," in a quieter voice because he's less happy and then the second part of that stanza, "I am the seal inside the sea and when I am away from land, my home is free inside the sea," in a louder and happier voice because that's where he feels at home and obviously happier.

Same Poem, Different Poem

The reminder students were given brings to mind Louise Rosenblatt's description of the poem as a highly personal experience: "a specific reader and a specific text at a specific time and place: change any of these, and there occurs a different circuit, a different event — a different poem."

Calkins, Lucy. 2003. *Poetry: Powerful Thoughts in Tiny Packages*. Portsmouth, NH: Heinemann.

Nadia reads the first stanza in the way she has just described. The others read along as they listen.

Miguel (*to Nadia*): I have a suggestion. To really show that he is happier in the sea, why don't we slow our reading of "my home is free inside the sea"? It would sound like this . . .

Miguel reads the entire stanza again and slows down for the last few lines as he has just described.

Britney: Yes, that's it. That sounds great. By slowing it down, you really feel how much it means to him to be back in the sea as a seal. Right?

There are nods of agreement around the table.

These students, along with those in other Readers theatre groups in the classroom, were in the process of refining their oral interpretations of text with the support of coaching, feedback, and modeling from each other while I roamed from group to group, offering support where needed.

Over the next few days, they continued to prepare and rehearse for their Readers theatre recording and performance the following week. In the end, our students divided the poem into four parts and rehearsed by reading and rereading the text aloud 10 to 15 times. Feedback and support for one another on topics such as expression, volume, phrasing, emphasis, and reading rate continued.

A few days before our students were set to perform their Readers theatre for their classmates and upload their recording to the class website, they audio-recorded their reading to listen for and discuss areas of strength and areas for improvement. Here is a portion of their dialogue:

Nadia: I think you sound so great. Britney, how you used your voice will really help the audience hear how scared the mother is when she sees the father's face and she knows it means her son will have to go back to the sea.

Miguel: I think I did a good job of sounding hopeful when the dad talks about teaching his son how to swim in the foam one day.

Britney (*to Miguel*): I think you also sounded sad when you said that part too, which is good because he was pretty sad when he had to wait to do that.

Nadia: Let's try and slow the whole thing down just a bit on our next try. I think it would sound even better.

Each of the students in our group nods enthusiastically in agreement.

With repeated reading opportunities embedded in its very practice, Readers theatre gave the students an authentic and enjoyable way to improve their fluency. Our students had opportunities to use language to express opinions and emotions, solve problems, make decisions, and socialize. Through this process, students began to see themselves as experts on the meanings of the words and sentences within *The Seal Child*. As experts, they began to make multiple decisions necessary for text interpretation and performance. With formative feedback provided during Readers theatre rehearsals, they were assisted by the teacher and one another to make deeper connections to text and to read with meaning and expression. Through this engaging and active process, students had repeated opportunities to explore reading, writing, listening, and speaking in meaningful ways. This served to sharpen our students' insight into the literature and ultimately infuse the words of the poem with meaning through their voices.

What better way to invite our students to be more engaged and motivated meaning-makers of a text, and to ultimately find and share the song that it sings!

CHAPTER 7

Writing as Response

Connecting our writing with our reading now seems to make sense to me. Of course, no matter the topic, we are always borrowing the bits of craft we remember from the texts we have read: it is one way writers grow. For years, I separated reading and writing in my teaching. Now I recognize the connections we can make to enable our students to find ideas in the texts they experience that may inspire them to write responses or to compose in a different genre or format.

Resources for Writing: Other Texts and Life Experiences

Students can look for fresh possibilities in the stories they read, borrow from them, remold them, and tell them anew. When they are immersed in stories, students develop a sense of narrative and how it works in all its forms. They become actively engaged in making meaning through language — the syntactic patterns, the idioms, the imagery, the multiple meanings of words. When students meet and use a variety of story structures and styles, they learn about genre and form. They know which sentences, which words, which images they want to remember and savor as they add the ideas, motifs, values, and language of the story to their own language storehouses, resources for their own written responses.

Valuing Life Stories

We need to encourage students to tell the stories of their own lives, the stories of their own making. For many of the students, this respect and understanding of story's central place in our lives may never have been fully valued.

When what they write is dependent upon another source, students have a resource that they can draw upon and that we can offer. This type of *dependent authorship* lets students look at their own work and at the work of the text all at once. When they interpret the text, add to the text, continue the text, or rewrite new understandings, they are involved in *shared authorship*. Rather than encouraging students to copy the text and become involved in plagiarism, we can find ways to both inspire and enable our students to make use of the texts of others as they create their own, not through memorization, but through reworking, retelling, and reliving them until they are deeply embedded in their own writing tool chests. They can be guided and inspired by other memorable text experiences told by significant tellers who matter.

Students can develop and share personal stories as responses to texts they have encountered. When they do so, young authors become aware that writing can reflect their lives. As they connect their lives with the texts, they can borrow the shapes and cadences, the words and phrases, of the professional authors whose works they have met.

Writing between, beyond, and alongside the lines

If student responses to their reading lead to intriguing questions, then there may be opportunities for the students to write about the happenings between the lines or develop the unwritten scenes. What drives my own work with students, though, are the analogous or parallel worlds that can be created alongside those in the story. What would another character do in a similar situation? How might a different action change the course of events in the new telling? As they consider the twists their questions bring to what they have read, students can create a new story on the shoulders of the original.

Weighing and expressing opinions

We want readers to carefully weigh evidence from a text in order to make thoughtful decisions regarding their own opinions, to combine textual information with their own background knowledge. Students need to draw conclusions and apply logical thought to substantiate their interpretations. They need to be helped to recognize persuasive writing and use judgment as they read it. They can draw upon issues from the texts they are experiencing, and develop and research information that deepens and supports their opinions. We want readers both to make and to recognize informed opinions.

Writing based on text-related inquiries

Students can write their own researched information using the text as the basis for their inquiries. Student inquiries and investigations can grow from the topics or issues generated by the text, the other responses, or the students' own interests and questions that cause them to want to find answers or solutions. Intensive long-term research projects immerse the students in authentic reading and writing experiences, and we can help maintain their interests and sustain their efforts.

Students often need help in planning how to structure the information they have found through their research inquiry. We can help them with ways to sort, select, and arrange their data. What's more, we need to offer guidance and models for building effective structures. In the end, we want to be able to see what they have learned through intensive research writing, and the results should document their growth. Occasions on which students present their inquiries can involve written and visual demonstrations of the research, as well as oral communication.

Writing with poetic voice

When students begin to observe poetic forms and to notice the affective side of language, they are coming to understand poetry as a special way of representing their "voice."

Students can write responses that use poetry structures to hold their affective thoughts and important ideas in a condensed and powerful way. Many of the young adult novels written today use free verse to tell the story, and these can act as models and demonstrate for students the strength of working with poetic forms to express their responses to a text.

Script writing from oral and print sources

It is not easy to write words that others can then give life to, but if script writing serves as a way of responding to a text, your students will gain experience. What's more, if you can create a process where the writers hear their words being spoken aloud and can then recognize the need for revision, the writing process is truly authentic. Script writing, including storyboards, is one of the best activities I have found for causing students to revise.

- Transforming a text selection into script dialogue involves students in several literacy processes. For example, selecting part of a novel and turning the narrative into dialogue forces careful reading of the text and requires the writer to interpret the prose, maintaining the intent of the story and the characters while presenting the thoughts and actions through dialogue. The script writing becomes a response activity.
- Partners could work on transforming a short story into a script. A page or two is usually enough text to write and revise. (How much narrative will they retain? How will they externalize the thoughts of the characters?) Groups can then exchange stories for reading aloud and sharing.
- Conversations that have been taped are good sources for scripting. An improvised scene can be transformed into a script for others to read aloud. It is important to keep the scenes brief: transcribing is hard work, but as James Moffett indicated, in his book with Betty Jane Wagner, *Student-Centered Language Arts and Reading*, these are perfect occasions for observing how the conventions of print work, as recorded speech has to be represented in print.
- A conversation recorded from a book club or a literature circle can be an excellent resource for transcribing into script. Students can select a significant moment in the discussion to be transcribed, and the resulting dialogue can be used by group members to analyze their contributions to the understanding of the novel read.

Moffett, James, and Betty Jane Wagner. 1976. *Student-Centered Language Arts and Reading, K to 13.* Boston: Houghton Mifflin.

Introduction to Demonstrations of Responding through Writing

Responding to a text through writing includes a variety of forms, from answering reflective questions to writing narratives in character. In many of the other modes discussed in this book, you will often find written expression as a medium of thought. In this section, we focus on the act of writing as a real response, as students consider their reading strategies, recount the original text from a new viewpoint, and create headlines for the folktale. We write to understand ourselves.

Four articles by teachers involved in the Selchie Project present classroom experiences in creating written responses.

REFLECTING ON THE STORY

Haroula Madones

In this article, Haroula Madones describes working with her Grade 2 class in Crescent Town Public School in Toronto.

I developed this three-stage approach to sharing the story *Seal Song* with my class:

- Before *Seal Song*
  Preview — look at cover, make predictions about what we think the story will be about. Look at the inside cover which shows a human changing to a seal and discuss what is happening in that image.
- During *Seal Song*
  Role on the Wall for Sheila [the selchie]: what we know — inside; what we want to know —outside.
- After *Seal Song*
  I read this quotation from the story to the students: *"Watch," said the oldest fisherman. "That child will never let salt water touch her skin. If it does, she*

must return to the sea.” Then I gave them two questions to think about from their own perspectives.

1. Sheila knew that if she touched water, she would turn into a seal forever. Why do you think she still decided to go into the sea?
2. Would you have reacted in the same way if you were Sheila?

Their answers, as the sampling below demonstrates, revealed their understanding of the conundrum Sheila faced in deciding whether to try to save her friend Finn.

Reyan

1. Sheila went into sea to resque Finn from thunderstorm and if she did not go into the water then she would lose her friend forever.
2. I will turn into a seal forever. Then I will not lose my friend forever. Then I would be a good friend. My friend would also like me. I will have magical powers to save my best friend.

Abiha

1. I think she went into the water even if she knew she would turn into a seal forever because she had to help her friend Finn. Finn couldn't hear anything, she said, and good friends always help their friend when their friend is in trouble and she would not want to lose her friend and if she was in trouble Finn would help her and she was treating others the way you want to be treated which is following the golden rule.
2. If my friend was in trouble I would go help him or her because I would not want to lose my friend and if I was in trouble my friend would help me. I would treat other the way you want to be treated!

Anika

1. I think Sheila dived in the sea because she knew that Finn could die and that she would probably be forbidden to go on land.
2. Well maybe because there is a good side and bad side. I would save my best friend but I'd be a seal forever. But I'd still be his friend.

Huan

1: Sheila wanted to help Finn even if she would turn into a seal forever because she was very worried about him and that he would die the same way she died when she got caught in a fisherman's net and Finn had saved her from her death.
2: If I was the girl that turned into a seal forever named Sheila, I would have reacted in the same way if I were

Sheila because I would be worried about him because of the storm and that he would die the same way I died when I got caught in a fisherman's net and Finn saved me from my very very, very horrible death

Daryl

1: To help Finn so he wouldn't die from the storm. Because I always want to help.
2. Yes, because I wouldn't want Finn to die from storm and I wouldn't care if I was a seal forever and ever and live in water. Plus, I like seals.

DIARY ENTRIES AS ANALOGOUS STORY

Rachael Swartz

Rachael Swartz teaches her Grade 7 class in Toronto.

I read the story "The Seal's Skin" aloud with all my Grade 7 students, and we had an in-role activity where they turned to talk in role with a partner. One partner took the voice of the fisherman, and the other student took the voice of another character. They had to speak about this question: "Did the couple make the right decision?" The focus was on voice and perspective. The enrichment assignment that I offered the students was to create a response where one character's point of view is expressed. It could take the form of a diary, letter, blog, comic strip, email, postcard, or whatever the student chose.

Daniel Romero, whose work is featured below, chose to create an imaginary character, Phil Wayne, with a pop-culture flavor to the language and setting he used to create his analogous story. He incorporated asides to the reader, some slang terms, and imaginative names for the crew to maintain the hurried pace of the dialogue, written with daily entries from his fishing boat. Yet inside his slightly flippant style, he finds ways to embed the original story's intent.

Day 369:

Like I said in 'Day 256' I'm just a fisherman who lives in New Orleans, and all I ever want is company, besides my lovely wife. I mean, a kid, a young spark-fly that can both make me laugh and cry. But I can't have one. But, I still like to sing a little lullaby-ish kind of song to my wife, Irene. And just so you don't have to go back to 'Day 1', my name is Phil Wayne. And I am from England and moved here to be a fisherman. Anyways, back to having a kid. I've always wanted a kid to, you know, bring to Baseball Games and for him to be a fisherman too. I would like to name my little chap either Alexander or Raphael (I always loved that name) and if it's a daughter then either Sally or Rosie. But like I said, I can't really have a girl or a boy. Well, my lunch hour is up, back to fishing and catching some Trout . . .

Day 371:

Sorry I couldn't write yesterday, a lot happened (Plus, my boss cut back my lunch break 20 minutes because some bloody idiot let out the lobster cage and I had to retrieve all the bloody lobsters, so I had to go through all that rub-bish) And now My boss is angry at me. Wait . . . Yup I was right, now I have to go. But like they say back in England, A Bag of Biscuits Won't Pay The Piper . . .

Day 372:

Well, I'm on my boat scouting the perimeters but I see something small and kind of grey. I think the proper shade is Koala Bear. Me thinks I should check it out. Well, now that I'm back I can explain it. It's a small grey seal. Poor little laddy must have got thrown off track now that the waves are rougher. Now that I'm writing here, I've real-ized: He doesn't have parents, and I don't have a child. He shall stay with a chap like me! Even though it's not a real lad, its close enough, I can raise it, feed it, it'll be just like having a real mate! I can't wait till I show Irene this little cute seal and see the look on her face! So, now I'm walk-ing home with a meter length seal in my arms, but now it's turning kinda brown-ish red like mahogany. It doesn't matter, because I'm here. I don't know what to exactly tell her so I'll just say "Nothing but a seal pup I found stranded in the shallows and longing for its own. I thought we could give it love and care until its old enough to seek its kin." So I start unraveling it and Irene is going mad! Now that I take another look at it, it's a real boy (Kind of like the old tale of Pinocchio) He had sparkling grey eyes (Which don't look all that bad, after all, female laddy's are suckers for eyes) and silvery grey hair and he smiling at me. Finally, the Bag of Biscuits Payed the Piper!

Day 373:

I was puzzled the fact a seal pup turned into a boy and I did some snooping around and with some research, I found out it was a "Selchie" a man upon the land and seals in the sea. It was a famous story back in London. Me and Irene also decided to never return him to the sea for he shall forever remain a man, so we can treat him like a boy of our own. My wife suggested we name him "Greyling" because of his eyes and hair is the color of a storm-coming sky. Like I said, it looked more like a Koala Bear shade, but this wasn't the book "Fifty Shades of Grey", this was the beginning of a new book in my life called "Fifty Shades of Greyling."

Day 586:

Hi, remember me? I didn't write in my diary anymore because I'm feeding and raising Greyling now. Now he's a 14 year old man. With full potential who sees the world differ-ently from when I picked him up on shore. He is a volunteer for me and my crew, he mends my nets and tended my boat, and he is even learning some seamanship! (Knots, ranks, boat parts, compass, throwing rope etc.) He really is a nice guy.

Day 588:

Yesterday was Greyling 15th Birthday! He really is going to get bloody strong and powerful. Oh, my boss is letting me write on my ship again, what a nice chap! I'm off at sea to find some more crabs for the Japanese restaurant in Colorado "Kura Japanese Restaurant". It is pretty stormy and these pages are going to get wet. It is a very bloody storm. I hope Irene is ok. The sky is now black and the fish look to have trouble moving their fins. Using a spare pair of binoculars I look to see if Irene and Greyling are fine. I just find a little hut on shore to be totally wiped out. I also see a lot of townspeople running toward the grey cliffs to avoid waters. I try to look for Greyling and Irene (It won't be hard to find Greyling with his hair) but I can't, I just hope their alright. Uh oh, our sails are flapping bloody fast! And our mast might brake let me just fix this! Whoa! The wind blew our whole supply of crabs!!! I don't care about some bloody crabs, me and my crews lives are a stake! (By the way, in case I forgot to say, I have 7 people on my boat: Jay "Blue" Sand, me, Dice "Trickster" Murphy, Hunter Mack, Ambrose Watoski, Wendell Shay, and Thomas Lopez) Great, just what the doctor ordered! Half the mast is broken! THE WIND PICKED IT UP WITH EASE! now I'm just hanging on to a broken pole! This doesn't look good; the sea currents took a piece of my ship! now I'm sinking with the hole!!! And to make things worse, IT'S BLOODY COLD!!!!!!! I hope somebody will save me.

Day 589:

Day 590:

Thankfully, I didn't sink, I'm just floating around in rough winds of change. My pages are soggy but my pen still has ink, I will just write slowly, Luckily, being a fisherman, I get thrown off my boat a lot so I learned to hold my breath for maximum 9 minutes. (David Blaine can for 18 minutes! I hope to get someplace around there) Hold on, I see something floating that looks like Greyling! It's coming closer... IT'S MY SON!! He picked me up and swam me to shore. It didn't even look like he gave an effort, he did it easily. I couched up some water and noticed Greyling wasn't with me, I scouted around but I saw Greyling and he didn't see me (He was facing the water, I faced Irene) He dived in and swam away. Irene was heartbroken. She couldn't bear to see Greyling had left us. But I could tell it was for the best. We cared for the young lad, now that he is older he must care for himself.

Day 1180:

It's been a year since we let Greyling go. But, once a year, the folks and mates across new Orleans report a grey seal around my home. And that has become a folk tale. Weirdly

enough, it's no ordinary seal, it is a young boy named Greyling. Who has come to tell his parents, me and Irene, about
his adventures underwater. And I listen and laugh and cry.
But, like I said, that's all I ever wanted a son for.

WRITING REFLECTIONS ON RECOGNIZING INFERENCES

Elizabeth Costa-DaMaia

Teacher Elizabeth Costa-DaMaia describes working with a Grade 4 class at St. Marguerite d'Youville Catholic Elementary School in Oakville, Ontario.

We had just completed a series of lessons on making inferences.

I took my students to the forest across the street for the first reading of *Greyling*. I asked them to just listen carefully and said that we were not going to discuss the story. I just wanted it to sink in and let the story muddle in their minds.

The next day, I read the fable in class and encouraged a Pair-Share activity, then a class talk session, where they led the discussion and I listened. The day after that we watched a YouTube video on what a storybook illustrator's goals are and then we discussed the video.

Next, I distributed copies of the story in print and asked them to use the graphic organizer we had been working with to respond to inferences they made while reading, where they reflect on text clues and their own schema to make an effective inference. They can then use these inferences to become effective illustrators. I was thinking of asking each student to reflect on inferences made, then choose their favorite part of the story to illustrate a scene that authentically responds to their own thoughts and inferences.

Making Inferences: The Greyling by Shaye (SELCHIE)			
	My Inference	Clues from the Text	My Schema
What can you infer about the husband and wife's relationship?	I think the relationship is strong and they love each other very much.	Because the fisherman does not want to make his wife sad.	because when people love them so much they don't want to hurt each other. Haven't you ever not told someone something to not hurt them.
What can you infer about the relationship between Greyling and his parents?	I think it's very strong they love him so much.	Because the mother loves Greyling so much but she wants to let him go to the sea. Plus the fisherman and the fisher man's wife want a baby so much.	I have parents and they love me very much. I do not keep secrets from them.
Make an inference about how Greyling is feeling during his first dive into the ocean.	I think Greyling felt free.	When the author described how he flowed through the water you could tell he felt free.	When I dive into the water relaxed and free, it feels like nothing can stop me.
How do you think the mother feels at the end of the story about letting her son go?	I think she felt sad but good and missed him very much. She will never forget him like a man would.	The book said that she "grabbed her son and clutched on to his ears" when the people said let him go save the drowning soul.	A mother would never let her son go. That is why mothers think it's so hard to let her son move out.
What message is the author trying to share about nature in this story?	The message the author is trying to share is nature can be good to you but when you mess with it, it could be bad.	The good part; they had moss on the hut that keep them warm in winter and cool in the summer. The bad thing — there was a storm because they took a seal and never gave it back.	A lot of movies including nature mention if you mess with nature this could happen to you. Also most of the world is polluted which means we messed with nature and now our world is not as safe as it could be.

This graphic organizer helped students, including Shaye, provide thoughtful, concrete responses.

Shaye's work shows Greyling's transformation from boy to seal as Greyling dives into the water to save his father.

RETHINKING THE STORY THROUGH WRITING ACTIVITIES

Theresa Merritt

The four response activities that Theresa Merritt developed were built around the students' reading of the selchie tale. They involved two classes of Grade 8 students at St. Marguerite d'Youville Catholic Elementary School in Oakville, Ontario.

When considering how students would best respond to *Greyling*, I thought first of how to meet curriculum demands and then of what would make the fable most meaningful to the students. Our writing pathway determined that writing genres, specifically a recount, were a priority for students.

1. RECOUNT FROM A POINT OF VIEW

As a whole class, we reviewed the key elements of a recount and co-created criteria for success. I guided the students towards recounting the storm scene as I also wanted them to focus on perspective, something with which they had previously demonstrated difficulty. They were asked to generate a recount based on one of four possible perspectives: (1) Greyling, (2) the fisherman, (3) the fisherman's wife, or (4) an onlooker.

This is the assignment as I worded it:

GREYLING: THE DAY OF THE GREAT STORM

Write a Recount of the great storm, from the first-person perspective of the young man Greyling (15 years old) as he stood atop the "great, grey cliff," the fisherman as he clung to the "broken mast" of the boat, the fisherman's wife as she "cried" for someone to save her husband, or one of the onlookers from the town who gathered on the cliffs to watch "the boy dive down into the sea."

The samples of student writing that follow represent the three main characters in the story.

WIFE'S PERSPECTIVE

I *can't* believe it my beloved husband, slowly sinking waiting for the dark sea to gulp him up. Worst part is no one will help him, People he's known for years, best friends, friends are just leaving him to die. While me and my son Greyling is waiting for a miracle to happen. so far none. Suddenly I hear my son 'I will save him mother' and he's gone before I can protest. I hear all the fishermen telling how he's a goner while I'm weeping away my sorrows. I watch my son dive in the cold evil water, watching the waves tare his cloths away from his body, I watch him reach my husband and swim him back to shore. Right then and there I ran as fast as my legs could carry me to my beloved husband. I look around and notice Greyling gone all that's left of him is his scattered clothes around the shore. All that were heard were the mumbles of how he was a brave man, but my husband and I both knew in side that he was not just a man but he was both man and seal.
Erin

FISHERMAN'S PERSPECTIVE

As I clung onto the broken wooden mast, I felt my heart sinking with it. Memories of Greyling and my wife brought tears that threatened to spill onto the unforgiving sea. Noticing I had sunk another couple feet, I scrambled to the top of my heart with my heart beating so loudly, I could feel it beating the side of my rib cage. Looking up at the cliffs, I saw Greyling, struggling against my wife's grasp. Attempting to raise my voice over the crashing waves, I yelled "no!" but, it fell to deaf ears. Accepting my fate, I closed my eyes and thought of Greyling. With a bitter smile, I recounted Greyling searching for sea shells, his stormy grey eyes scanning the tide pools, his wide smile when he found a "pretty" shell and his joy when he saw it displayed on the mantel. A small tear ran down my cheek, despite my desperate attempts to stop it. I opened my eyes abruptly when I felt something nudge the mast, almost throwing me right off. With a heavy heart, I forced myself to look down at the great grey seal, staring up at me with the grey eyes I had grown accustomed to over the years he grew up in my home. Finally, I let go, and let Greyling nudge me to the shore. I stared after him, and could swear he winked at me with those grey eyes of his, before diving back into the ocean.
Jennifer

An uneasy feeling fell upon me, as the sky turned dull, everyone in the villages were evacuating to the great, grey cliff. That's when it hit me, a storm was coming. I quickly rushed to the top of the cliff, where all the villagers were gathered, including my mom. As I approached to the crowd, I listened to what my mom said. As she was weeping and struggling, I heard those words that made my heart tremble and panic. My father was drowning, I rushed to the top, as I stood there and took a glance at the enormous ocean, only to find the day in my life I feared the most, the day my father would die. But at the same time, while looking at the wide blue ocean, I felt a deep need to go there and swim, as I recounted and remembered I never went to the sea. But this feeling was stronger than before, my heart ached and urged to enter it, and swim through it.

After several minutes, when I couldn't bear the guilt any longer, I offered myself to save my dad to the villagers, as I had this feeling that would change my life forever. My mom begged me to stay, but I still walked to the top and the edge of the great, grey cliff. I looked down at the waves crashing into the cliff, in an overwhelming feeling of anxiety and fear mixed up. I prepared myself to a jumping position; I didn't hesitate at all, and closed my eyes for a moment. As I opened them, I jumped from the great latitudes, towards what my heart desired the most; the sea.
Manuel

2. PERSPECTIVES ON AUTHOR PURPOSE

After they completed the recount, I put students in groups, according to their particular adopted perspective, point of view, or voice, and asked them what they thought the author was trying to teach us. These are the responses from the two Grade 8 classes:

Greyling's perspective
Class 1, Group 1: "Family is worth sacrifices, even your life, and even when the outcome can't be anticipated."
Class 2, Group 1: "Taking risks for the ones you love can pay off in the end."

Fisherman's wife's perspective
Class 1, Group 2: "You can find hope and love in someone you least expect, and in the end it will all turn out."
Class 2, Group 2: "You have to let your child be who they really are. Let them choose their own strength."

Fisherman's perspective
Class 1, Group 3: "If you love something, let it be free. Love is stronger than any storm."
Class 2, Group 3: "Be thankful for what you have."

Town onlooker's perspective
Class 1, Group 4: "Everyone needs the freedom to be who they really are. Their love will bring them back."
Class 2, Group 4: "Situations are not always as they appear."

3. MAIN IDEA IN A PHRASE

Students were randomly assigned to groups and asked to generate headlines, again in an effort to strengthen their understanding of main ideas. We reviewed what constitutes an effective headline and co-established criteria for success.

HEADLINES: EXAMPLES

Love in Action: Family's Love Goes a Long Way
Hybrid Child Saves Father from Storm
Strange "Grey Boy" Saves Father from Storm
Seal or Saviour?
Love for Father Greater Than the Sea
Ship Sunk in Storm of Season

4. DANCING THEIR UNDERSTANDING

Finally, students were offered an opportunity for free interpretation and focus related to *Greyling*. The only predetermined criterion was a review of what constitutes an effective dance performance. The only condition of group formation was that each group would have one member who had received some dance training in the past or present to help ensure that the groups were somewhat equal. The dance performance, again, was in line with the curriculum. However, this, by far, led to the most powerful, innovative, and applied transference of their understanding of the fable, as suggested in the photograph below.

CHAPTER 8

Responding through the Arts

I See What You Mean (2nd edition), by Steve Moline, is filled with insights and techniques for helping students to both explore visual texts and construct them as responses to topics, issues, and information texts. Graphic and artistic power can open up such new and deep understanding.

For readers of any age, the arts are part of the serious business of making meaning: they partner with words for communicating our inner thoughts and feelings. For example, what relationship exists between the visual and the verbal in picture books? Could one stand without the other? Do they tell the same story? Students of all ages can draw and paint along with their writing and their responses to text — representing ideas through visual and graphic art is not just for those who can't write fluently, and creating pictures is more than rehearsal for real writing. A simple drawing of a poignant moment in the story speaks volumes about the student's reaction to a text.

In the arts today, we see multimodal creations, where sound and music can be an important part of meaning making in a visual context such as film or possibly tableaux. These interconnected modes can contribute to mood and help engage the viewer-listeners, allowing a stronger emotional and thoughtful response. Conversely, students do not necessarily have to be experienced musicians to use sound and music as a response, as the article "Musical Storytelling" establishes.

Arts and Media — A Rich Range of Modes

We want students to move beyond the literal in their responses, to use the elements of design and media to delve into deeper interpretations of the text they are exploring. Students can also select, shape, and present ideas and feelings through a variety of art forms and materials, expressing inventive and innovative ideas, finding satisfaction in making and creating artistic products, becoming emotionally and intellectually engaged, and more willing to revise, shape, and work towards improving and completing their creations. They can incorporate a variety of multimedia and technology in their compositions; they can also transform ideas represented in one art form into another composition. Finding different modes for constructing and composing their ideas can motivate them and give them form for expressing their own unique voice.

Art, sound, and graphic activities may include the following:

- transforming a poem into a song;
- finding a CD to accompany an interpretive dance;
- adding sound narration to a PowerPoint;
- putting written texts online with accompanying voices;
- constructing a visual timeline or a story map;
- illustrating what students believe is the most powerful moment in a story;
- creating masks for dramatizations;
- representing scenes through still images, or tableaux;
- using a graphic comic-strip program to comment upon the ideas in the text;

- writing a personal picture book patterned after or suggested by the story;
- filling their journals with their artwork, expressing their thinking, observations, ideas on assessments and revisions, descriptions of process, future plans, and reflections on their learning;
- selecting words they met while reading a book, playing with the words and their shapes, illustrating them, writing them in calligraphy, or creating three-dimensional effects;
- using drawing as an intermediary step between reading a text and discussing it in small, art-sharing groups, where other members can speculate on the artist's intent before listening to the interpretation;
- using graphic organizers so that students can represent their thoughts;
- working with Venn diagrams to represent comparisons and contrasting information within one story or book (e.g., settings) or between two or more books;
- responding to ideas and feelings generated by the text through visual art; and
- using other media to represent the text, for example, iMovies, video, or films; or locating art reproductions that relate to the text.

Plot organizers help students summarize a plot and understand its organization. They also act as models for students writing their own stories.

Introduction to Demonstrations of Responding through the Arts

The teachers involved in the following demonstrations of the selchie stories incorporated a wide variety of visual and aural modes into their student responses. In looking at the student work in other modes, we can see that visuals as responses are represented almost every time. Somehow, the need to express through drawing and painting lasts throughout the school years, and we now can recognize these as texts that hold meaning, that signal thoughtful imaginations at work, stimulated by the tale. You will also read about clay sculptures and musical interpretations, along with tableaux of children retelling events taken from the story or poem. Two classes incorporated an integrated arts approach as responses to the selchie people. Arts matter!

ARTIFACTS AND SCULPTURE

Paul Stewart

Arts educator Paul Stewart describes working with a Grade 6 class and teacher in a school in Toronto.

The use of clay sculpture to allow students to interpret the story "The Seal's Skin" was a collaborative effort by the classroom teacher and myself. A visiting clay artist, I had been conducting Ontario Arts Council–funded clay workshops with all of the classes in this particular school. The participating students for this project came from a Grade 6 class in a culturally mixed, primarily low-income, working-class neighborhood in Toronto's Central East end.

When my wife, a teacher educator, told me that David's book was being assembled, I asked the teacher of the Grade 6 class if we could try the clay response to the story "The Seal's Skin." I had used clay mask-making in conjunction with story development and as a response to student-written poetry before but never clay sculpture as a response to a given story.

Four days before the sculpting day, the teacher read the students the story. This sharing was followed by a class discussion of what the story meant to them. The discussion was fairly superficial, mainly focused on clarifying the story. When I learned that the initial discussion had been quite limited, I asked the teacher to have a second discussion to see whether the students could explore the story more deeply. The classroom teacher led this further discussion the day before the clay workshop. Although understanding of the story deepened, the teacher felt that the students still weren't engaging much with the ideas and emotions in the story.

On the morning of the clay workshop, I told the story orally and explained the technical issues that the students would need to consider when working with clay. I reinforced that the students should spend their lunch reviewing the story in their minds with the purpose of choosing a scene or an image to create in a clay sculpture. The students seemed apprehensive at this point. They were worried that they wouldn't be able to think of anything.

CHOOSING AND REPRESENTING A SCENE

After the lunch period the students came to a spare classroom being used as a clay workshop room and were given further sculpting instructions and their tools and clay. The students were free to represent any aspect of the story using the clay. The only limitation was that they would all work with an oval disk of clay about 12 cm by 15 cm (5" by 6") as a base for the project. The workshop lasted two hours.

I learned a great deal by listening in to student conversations during the creation of the sculptures and by chatting with the students while they worked. As they made their pieces, I could see their ideas solidify. They seemed to come to a growing understanding of what they were trying to portray with the clay. When they began, many were at a loss as to what they wanted to produce. Some had considerable difficulty choosing what to make. Others knew immediately what they wanted to make and how to do it. Even those who had a strong image they wanted to create refined their ideas during the creation of their pieces.

Some chose to use the disk as a face mask, others built the fisherman's cottage with or usually without people, one built a boat with the fisherman in it and the selchie swimming around it. Several students created the cave mouth with the selchie skins outside. One chose to construct a sculpture of the fisherman alone on the disk with no other ornamentation (see the art images on the next page). This student explained that when the selchie left him, the fisherman was completely alone. I found it interesting that this particular student, though at a table with three peers, said almost nothing to anyone else during the workshop. He, too, was much alone, it seemed.

I noticed patterns in what the students chose to create. For example, of a class of about 20 students, four created the cave, and all four were girls. Only one girl made clay figures representing the selchies. The other three girls made only a cave, two with selchie skins. On the other hand, all of the students who created the fisherman or his house were boys.

SCULPTURES AS EXPRESSIONS OF UNDERSTANDING

During the clay workshop the teacher videotaped individual students. The teacher asked them to explain their clay sculpture and what it represented. In watching these video recordings, I was surprised how the students seemed to overlay the original story with elements not in the story. One who created a mask of the fisherman described it as follows: "My piece is about the fisherman who was mad at the sea woman for taking the seal skin that he found." This student did acknowledge later that he could understand why the selchie had taken her skin back. Another boy also created a mask of the angry fisherman. Yet another student produced a mask of the fisherman, whom he described as surprised and sad. I was surprised that not one child created a representation of either the selchie's children in the sea or the selchie and fisherman's children on land.

A number of masks showed the sadness of the selchie. One interesting mask was split down the middle, with one half showing the sad selchie having left her children on land and the other half showing the sad selchie missing her children at sea.

There is no doubt that the use of clay helped these students to understand the story more deeply. The interviews that the teacher conducted with the students about their clay creations demonstrated that the clay had provided a way for the students to more fully engage with the story and its characters.

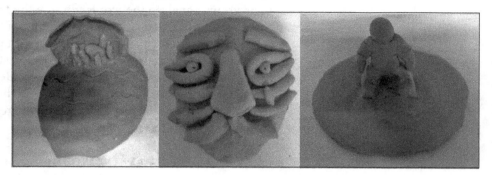

Three interpretations in clay, all using one oval disk: the cave with selchie skins, a face mask, the fisherman alone

MUSICAL STORYTELLING

Tony Nam-Hai Leong

Tony Nam-Hai Leong describes working with a Grades 9 and 10 Instrumental Strings class in Scarborough.

Ontario Ministry of Education Curriculum for the Arts — Grades 9–10. 2010. http://www.edu.gov.on.ca/eng/curriculum/secondary/arts910curr2010.pdf.

After reading "The Great Silkie of Sule Skerry" for the first time, I was immediately intrigued and excited at possible connections this ballad would have as a vehicle to teach my music classes.

As I reviewed the Ontario Arts Curriculum to see how I could connect this exercise to curricular expectations, I noticed that the curriculum encourages music teachers in Grades 9 and 10 to "identify and describe shared and unique characteristics of types of music from around the world; what are some ways in which a film score composer can engage a movie audience?" (p. 107). In addition, the curriculum also challenges us to have students "apply the creative process when performing notated and/or improved music" (p. 102).

My high-school Instrumental Strings music class had been studying the differences between programmatic music, which has an implied narrative, and absolute, or non-representational, music, and I thought this would be a fantastic opportunity for them to take the words of "The Great Silkie of Sule Skerry" and provide a soundtrack, using and exploring non-traditional sounds with their stringed instruments to accompany the text. I had done this exercise in a different context a few years back for Curriculum Canada Services to highlight the new Ontario Arts Curriculum.

DEVELOPING NON-TRADITIONAL SOUNDTRACKS

I started the lesson by playing the students a quick clip from a movie with the sound turned off. As a class, we generated thoughts about the role that music

Check out the 2010 webcast, *Learning through the Arts: Exploring Non-traditional Sounds*, at http://www.curriculum.org/arts/nontraditional.shtml.

and sounds have on the overall affect, or mood, of movies and potentially, text. The students quickly noticed and commented on how disengaged they were to the movie without the audio — and how bored they were becoming. "Sir, it was hard to know what was going on in the movie with the sound turned off" (Grade 9 student). "I became distracted by sounds from outside because there wasn't anything going on in the movie" (Grade 10 student).

I then introduced "The Great Silkie of Sule Skerry" and told the students that since they realized how sound provides another dimension to text and film, they would be responsible for finding and creating the sound effects for the text in this poem. Since "The Great Silkie of Sule Skerry" consists of five verses, I decided to divide my class into five groups. Students were asked to read through the text in their groups, analyze the words, discuss the text's meaning, and identify words that explain the mood and summarize the content.

Students were then asked to come up with different sounds on their stringed instruments to describe in an aural representation the words. For example, they might tap on the back of the instrument or slide rapidly back and forth on strings. At the same time, they were to keep in mind the five elements of music and apply dynamic and pitch changes, using different areas of the instruments to achieve a variety of colors and so forth.

NOTATING AND POLISHING SOUND COMPOSITIONS

In order to replicate these sounds, students were asked to devise a notation system so that others would be able to follow their score.

After spending some time working on this, students were invited to present a rough draft of their soundtrack. One member of their group would read the paragraph and the others would provide the soundtrack. Other members of the class gave feedback to the students on their rough draft.

Students were given time to rework, change, add, and enhance their soundtrack to perform it for the rest of the class as part of a presentation of the entire poem. One person from each group read the poem text while the other members provided the soundtrack. After the presentation, group members explained their notation so that another group could replicate their performance.

It was encouraging to see the level of excitement from the groups' performances. I felt that everyone became much more engaged because they had no inhibitions about creating new sounds on their instruments — technical expertise was not an issue. In addition, there was a general sense of ownership, as the compositions were something that they had created, not pieces composed by someone else. These are some comments my students made after their performances:

> "It was so much fun and easy finding new sounds on my cello." (Grade 9 cellist)

> "I found that by scraping the strings on the violin, it made a scary sound." (Grade 9 violinist)

> "I am going to pay more attention to the sound effects in movies now." (Grade 10 bass player)

> "We actually got to present our sound effects composition to the rest of the class. It was so cool doing it with the poem. It made the words come alive." (Grade 10 violist)

> "I wanna try finding some sound effects for movies at home." (Grade 9 violinist)

SOUNDS OF CREATIVE FREEDOM

I found this exercise extremely beneficial on many levels. In my observations, students were engaged and excited, as they were able to relate to and reflect on soundtracks for movies they had seen. In addition, I noticed that those students who normally struggled with the technical aspects of the stringed instrument felt engaged and contributed ideas more openly as there were no inhibitions to them creating sounds, using made-up techniques. Furthermore, I felt that the exercise provided a level of differentiated instruction. Some groups were able to be more complex in their compositions, adding more sound effects and complexity in their musical elements, while other groups were more basic in their structure.

INTEGRATED ARTS AS A MULTIMODAL EXPERIENCE

Wendy Agnew

Wendy Agnew is a Montessori educator in Kitchener who has worked with students in different classrooms as an arts resource teacher. In this article, Wendy describes a variety of arts experiences she organized for different groups of children in the elementary grades. A hallmark of her work lies in the choices she negotiates with her students as to how they will respond to the story.

After reading "The Seal's Skin," we decided to explore transformation by creating our own story of skins using the totem pole we were building, incorporating drama and art. This is what transpired.

DAY 1: DEVELOPING A STORY DRAMA

I read "The Seal's Skin" to a class of six- and seven-year-olds and asked them how we could respond. Several children wanted to draw pictures with chalk pastel, and they stayed in our portable to do so. The rest wanted to act the story with skins and use the totem pole to create a cooperative story inspired by "The Seal's Skin." We went outside with carpets, skins, totem pole, and a "seal."

The story veered wildly into themes I could not have imagined — children taking turns to shift it with their narratives. I have included their reflections so you can get a sense of another layer of "The Seal's Skin."

Q: WHAT DID YOU LIKE ABOUT OUR STORY DRAMA?

"The Sea Witch's Funeral."
"When the animals turned into people when the witches were fighting."
"When the animals turned back to stone again."
"When the seal was put on the totem."
"When the seal was sacrificed."
"I liked when the witches found out they were sisters."
"I liked when me and N found out that all the animals were our children."

Q: HOW DID READING "THE SEAL'S SKIN" AFFECT US?

"So we read the story and we took the transformation part and we made a different story with the skins."
"We read the story inside and we changed it with the skins outside."
"The totem is where death is supposed to be."
"The totem also helps things change into other things."
"There was two sadnesses in both stories."
"We had to face danger."

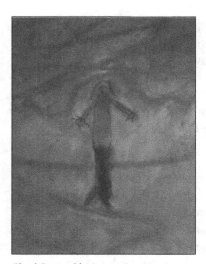

"Seal-Person" by L, age 7

"There was a gigantic earthquake and a flood and a funeral for the seal who we turned back to life with the totem pole."
"Without the totem we wouldn't be alive."

In this unit, a specially built totem pole played a key role in furthering the theme of transformation.

DAY 2: VISUALIZING AND PLAYING A GAME

I read the story to 12-year-olds — with their eyes closed. Here are some of their responses:

> "That was the best story ever."
> "It made me happy and sad at the same time."
> "I don't feel sorry for the guy because he stole her skin and even though he fell in love with her he didn't give it back."
> "That's selfish."
> "But you have to sacrifice stuff for love."
> "Abnegation is selflessness."
> "He was doing it for her love . . ." [A big debate transpired.]
> ". . . He would have showed her the skin and told her the truth and if she loved him enough she would have stayed."
> "Love, trust, betrayal . . . not clean."

Some of the class chose to create a game that involved transformation. They brainstormed and then mimed the game while I as the teacher narrated. Here is an excerpt:

> "We have a chest . . . and children." "The children can't open the chest, but they are all looking for the key but only the wife can open the chest to get the skin . . ." ". . . and I have an idea to add to F's . . . they can transform using animal powers, like a hamster can tunnel under the ground. They have to overcome obstacles by skins." "I have another idea from E's . . . the seal skin is locked up but it brings everyone together . . ."

I read the story to nine-year-olds. They made pictures in their minds while listening, and then brought the images to life through movement.

> "I can imagine the seal swimming around the boat — a red boat that's a canoe, and a grey seal and water."
> "I can imagine what the father would feel like to be betrayed."
> "I imagine the seal when they cut the skin off — imagine her turn into the girl and start crying. There would be sparkles."
> "She would be crying sparkles because she was magical."
> "When I was imagining the house and the sea, I was imagining the portable. The bed was over there and the chest was where the board is and the sea was out the windows."

IMAGINING A FILM: CREATING SCRIPTS

Andrea Kernius

Andrea Kernius describes her creative work in a self-contained Gifted classroom for students in Grades 1 and 2 at Sam Sherratt Public School in Milton, Ontario.

When I came across the story of the selchie, I knew my young students would love to hear it. My students love to be read to, and they have quite vivid imaginations. I decided to introduce the story by reading *Greyling*, by Jane Yolen.

Before reading the story, I asked my students if they had ever heard about selchies. To my surprise, not one of them had. I decided to let them discover selchies for themselves. During the first reading, the students simply listened. For the second reading, I gave them the task of visualizing the story. They made quick sketches to help them process and remember it. The next step was to create a script for a movie version of the story.

One student created this graphic retelling of the tale in 12 panels.

91

Picture, with poem text below, focuses on Greyling saving his dad.

The Greyling

The Greyling, the Greyling, the
    wonderful Greyling
He helped his Dad when he
    needed saving
half seal, half man.
He will do what he can,
half man, half seal.
He morphs and skin peels.
The Greyling, the Greyling, the
    wonderful Greyling.

Lori Belford teaches a Grade 3/4
Gifted class at Sam Sherratt Public
School in Milton, Ontario.

MAKING MODERN ANALOGIES

I was impressed by how the students modernized the story by adding and modifying certain characters. In one version, students changed the fisherman in the story to a "surfer dude." In this story, the "surfer dude," Joe, was looking for a wife to "fill his heart with love and joy." Joe meets the selchie, Shimmer, and falls in love. He asks her on several dates, all of which go terribly wrong (Joe takes Shimmer to a seafood restaurant and to a movie that starts out with a dead seal). The message for this movie is "if you love something, set it free." Joe learns that he cannot hold on to Shimmer after a surfing lesson goes wrong, and Shimmer goes back to the sea.

MESSAGES FROM GREYLING TO HIS HUMAN PARENTS

The final task for my students was to imagine that they were Greyling, the selchie who had been rescued by the fisherman and his wife in Yolen's version. I gave them the following prompt to respond to:

> Imagine that you are the selchie, Greyling, and you have returned to the sea. What would you say to your human parents (the fisherman and his wife) on land?

Many of the students focused once again on the lesson they felt the story was meant to share: "If you love something, set it free." One student wrote: "I want you to learn a lesson: If you like something, let it go! You did the right thing." I found it interesting that many of the responses mentioned the fact that they (as Greyling) had made friends in the sea. Many also mentioned how grateful they were to the fisherman and his wife for taking the seal pup in.

Some students painted their responses, using images to express their feelings about the story. One child, Bryceson, provided both picture and poem (text provided).

My students so enjoyed using *Greyling* by Jane Yolen as the basis for many of the responses we completed in class. I heard from many of the parents how excited their child was to tell them about the mythical creatures known as selchies.

VISUALIZING AND REPRESENTING THE STORY OF GREYLING

Lori Belford

I shared the printed text of the story *Greyling* with the students, and they immediately wondered aloud about the images that came into their minds. I had copies of the story for them to work with, and they set about illustrating their own versions of the folktale, using different styles and formats. They had enjoyed the story, but they thought that illustrations would be a bonus to their understanding of the text. Some students wrote words and drew images, some used a collage-style response, and others created diagrams to demonstrate the transformation from human to seal.

THE SEAL CHILD

The story is telling you the Seal man has two lives. One
on land and one in the sea. On the land he has a loving

mother, a soft bed, a sunny beach, and lots of sun. And in the Sea he can swim freely, he has a loving father, he can be a seal, he can have a different life with a new feeling. He has a life in each world he adores and can always love both parents. (*Grace*)

SEAL SKIN

This girl is a selchie. A selchie is a person on land but a seal in water. They shed their seal skin, then go to land. No-one knows if selchies are real. Personally, I think it is a old folklore from Scotland. I also think this photo is good because . . .
Selchies can be a girl or a boy, they live with seals and live in the ocean.
More information about selchies are:
• they eat fish like humans do and seals do,
• they like mermaids.
(*Ella*)

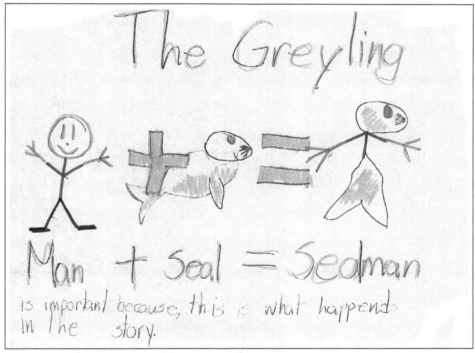

One student's representation of Greyling's transformation

SEAL SONG: FRIENDSHIP IN TABLEAUX

Hillary Cook-Thompson

Hillary Cook-Thompson teaches at Crescent Town Public School in Toronto.

We took our Grade 1 class to the valley and read them *Seal Song* by Andrea Spalding with illustrations by Pascal Milelli. The students chose to create their reading responses in the form of tableaux. They understood the theme of the book to be friendship. The students worked in groups to create tableaux that demonstrated

Students in Hillary Cook-Thompson's Grade 1 class worked with Seal Song *in the Don Valley.*

various forms of friendship. We took pictures of the students performing their tableaux and the different ways they showed friendship. Together, we also wrote a response about making our tableaux and made an art piece, using watercolors to create an ocean scene and then adding book characters chosen by the children.

"In the valley we read the book 'Seal Song.' We worked in groups and made tableaus on friendship. My tableau was about friens playing sucr." *(Andreas)*

"In the valley we read a book called 'Seal Song.' After we read the book we did an activity that was about 'friendship.' We worked in groups. My tableau was about helping a person from a fire. My group had three girls and two boys. I had a great time in the valley because it was helping nature by building an ant bridge and we had fun." *(Amad)*

"In the valley we read the book cold 'Seal Song.' We worked in groups and made tableaus on frendship. my tableaus was abut frends runing. It was so much fun." *(Kareem)*

Kareem drew this image of friends running together above her pencilled text on a simple line master, with lines for printing.

CREATING PICTURE BOOKS

David Booth with Eddie Ing

Eddie Ing teaches at Howard Park Public School in Toronto.

Eddie Ing built a unit around the story *Greyling* with his combined Grades 1 and 2 students. They listened to the tale and became involved in several activities exploring the issues, the setting, and the characters. Eddie's program involves writing as the heart of the learning, and his students produce amazing compositions, both in printed text and in visual arts. But it is in the interaction and combination of these artistic constructs where the abilities and voices of the children shine brightest.

In one of many responses, two boys, Lucas and Jack, portrayed the tale in 17 pictures, with text written by the teacher. Beyond retellings, students built a replica of the village where Greyling lived, with the houses below the cliff and the father's boat in the bay.

During this unit, the children retold the story in a myriad of ways. They lived through the tale with their oral retellings as a class, in groups, with a partner, and as individuals. They wrote about incidents in the story, adding dialogue and emotional moments of narrative. They also retold the story in word and image as a class, with each child contributing part of the story in writing and painting.

As his contribution to the composite picture book, Weini created a chart that shows the selchie from birth to adulthood.

PRINT ARTIFACTS FROM THE COMPOSITE PICTURE BOOK

After Phoebe drew her picture for the composite picture book, she wrote two letters in role:

Phoebe's picture shows the woman on the cliff, thinking of the boy.

Fri, June 13, 14
Dearest my love, Emily
I have just sipped my gulp of water.
I will use this bottle to put
my letter for you in it. I hope and pray
this letter reaches you safely.
I am scared and terrified that
I am going to die in this storm.
My mast is broken I have no more water
to drink and no more food to eat.
The boat has a hole in it and water
is leaking in. Please give Greyling a hug and kiss
and tell him that
I will love him forever.
I hope and pray that I will see you again.
Love from your husband,
James

Fri, June 13, 14
Dear My True Love, James,
Today I am really sad. I am sad because
you might be lost forever at sea.
I am so thankful of the love
you have shown me for all my life, James.
My happiest day was when you brought home
our son, Greyling. I finally got a baby boy
that we both loved together.
I pray for you to come home to me.
I love you very much.
Your wife
Emily

AN IMAGE OF SADNESS

Mairead Stewart

Since I wanted to demonstrate the wide range of choices of response modes in this book, I asked Mairead Stewart if she would participate. At the time, she was a Grade 11 student studying at a school for the arts in Toronto. Mairead chose to create an art piece that captured the soul of the folktale. Here, she describes her creative process.

For my response to "The Seal's Skin," I decided to draw how I felt about the story. My drawing is of the woman in seal form looking up at her daughter on one of her visits to see the children. I chose this particular image because my first response after reading the story was to wonder about the children and how they coped with everything. I wondered what they thought of their mother's sudden disappearance, and whether their father ever told them the whole story.

I guessed that the father hadn't told the children every detail because it was too painful for him to relive. Instead, the children figured out what happened on their own, and were able to sneak out to visit their mother when their father was away.

For me, this story was very sad. Everyone in the story ended up losing out in some way or another. The children lost their mother, the father lost his wife, and the woman lost her whole family. There were slight glimmers of a happy ending, though, and so I tried to show that in my drawing. Even though the mother lives in the sea, she is still able to visit her children and husband, and give them interesting things she finds. All in all, I really liked the story but wished it had a happier ending or a better message connected to it.

96

STUDENT PICTURE BOOK: "THE GREYLING"

Cameron Smith

Cameron Smith is a student who enjoys drawing and illustrating. Having read the story *Greyling* by Jane Yolen, the print version without pictures, he decided to retell the story in his own words and accompanied by his illustrations to create a picture book. Here is a sampling of pages from the Grade 7 student's book.

Act 1

Once upon a time, there was a fisherman and his wife. The sea was a big part of there life. They lived by the sea, and all they ate came out of the sea, and most of the fisherman's day was on the sea. They had a hut that was covered in moss so they kept warm in the winter and cool in the summer. There life looked good and they had every thing they needed and wanted... except a baby. Every sunrise and sunset the fisherman's wife would cry at the fact that she did not have a baby. This was the same with the fisherman but he hid it because he had it in his head that if he was not sad his wife would move on.

Act 9

Three months later the fisherman and his wife were living in a new hut that was covered with the finest moss to keep them warm in the winter and cool in the summer. Every year a seal would come up to the beach in front of the fisherman's house. The fisherman and his wife would let the seal come into there house. Now the town people thought this was odd. What they did not know was that this was no ordinary seal. It was Greyling coming home to tell them of stories of new lands and adventures on the open sea.
                    THE END

REPRESENTING "THE SEAL'S SKIN"

John Esposito

John Esposito teaches Grade 12 students English and Writer's Craft at St. Michael Catholic Secondary School in Stratford, Ontario.

Although this particular narrative genre (folklore) is not the standard fare of our Grade 12 University Prep curricula, I think it nonetheless provides a very valuable experience for my "war-weary" English and Writer's Craft students preparing for final exams and summative activities, respectively.

Whether they explore the "poetic" and, on occasion, "tedious" (their words) dramatic narratives of Shakespeare (they recently attended *King Lear* featuring Colm Feore); or whether they examine First Nations issues (Aboriginal and Icelandic mythology make a great "bridge"), students have the opportunity of tackling and responding to literature that not only expands their literary boundaries but also enriches their appreciation of the human condition. We remind our students that, above all else, it is the story that will enable the storyteller to succeed.

Over a three-day period, my Grade 12 students participated in an experimental workshop, called the Selchie Project, based on the folktale "The Seal's Skin," and it connected beautifully to our literature studies this term.

On Wednesday, I presented an introduction to the project to the students. Many of them were familiar with First Nations mythology, and several had a passing knowledge of family/ethnic folktales. However, few of them could find any significance or purpose in celebrating folktales beyond "childhood."

On Thursday, working in groups of three and four, the students continued their collaboration while I recorded their discussions and responses. Their goal was to create presentations that they would share with the rest of their classmates on Friday.

The brief album that follows will allow you to glimpse and encounter my students' activities. (I did not include the original song and comic strip because of size limitations.) I hope you will find our three-day exploration of "The Seal's Skin" both interesting and useful.

STUDENT WRITING SAMPLES FROM THE FOLKLORE PROJECT

IN MY OWN WORDS

I was free once, the water my companion as I spent my days between the waves. Then they came, the tall men with their shiny, pointed spears. They came all at once, too many to out-swim even with our sleek tails. They surrounded us, grabbed us, pulled us from our watery home. They took us to shore, and greedy hands pulled at our skins. They took them from us, our key to the sea, and left us heaping and broken in a cave, unable to move although our skins sat only outside.

That's when I first saw him. He peered around as he approached, but could not see me tucked away in the cave. He reached for the skins, *my skin*, stroking its soft fur. I tried to call out, to tell him to leave it alone, but no air could reach my lungs. He took my skin, still caressing it, and wandered back the way he came without ever noticing I was there. If I could have, I would have cried. But no tears came to these new, earth-bound eyes of mine. My hopes dropped to a previously unknown level.

I sat, staring, for what seemed like a lifetime. When the sun began to go down, I dragged myself out of my sheltered cave and onto the rock where my skin once lay. I stared out to the sea, my home, and tears began to fall down my cheeks. I heard something beside me, a shifting of sand. A man approached, cautiously. It was too dark to see his face, but from what I could see he looked kind, gentle. He stretched out his hand, and I took it.

NOT MY WORLD

Once a part of the sea,
I relished the cold water
On my skin,
The feeling of weightless-
  ness.

Soon a new danger made
  itself known,
My family was lost,
My skin was taken,
And I emerged in a new
  world.

Then my love found me,
He clothed me, nurtured
  me
And taught me about this
  new world.
Such a terrible world,
Such a beautiful world,
But not my world.

A constant search for my
  skin,
A reminder of what I had
  lost,
Consumed my thoughts
Consumed my dreams.

I soon grew to love this
  world,
It became my home,
And my new family.
My husband was so kind
  to me,
My seven bairn a part of
  me,
And so my search ended.

One day the gold gleam
Of my husband's secret,
Of his betrayal,
Made itself known.
Without a second
  thought,
I returned to my world,
My love's deception
Fresh in my mind.

Although my heart still
  aches,
And tears sting my eyes,
I cannot turn my back
On my love
And my bairn.

The PowerPoint images on page 100 capture the range of creative activities in which students in The Folktale Project took part.

Responding

Storyboarding

Blocking

Playing

Writing

Reflecting

Noting

Reciting

CHAPTER 9

Responding through Role-Play

Dramathemes, fourth edition, by Larry Swartz, includes dozens of techniques for engaging students in role-playing activities through games and improvisations, and these can apply to any text the students are exploring. Students can enter a text in role and gain a new understanding of the motivations and behaviors of characters they encounter.

Young children engage in role-play from their beginning years. Their play times are filled with occasions for becoming workers, other family members, and characters from television and books. Role-play lets children leave the narrow confines of their own worlds and try out new forms of identity. When students take part in structured role-playing situations, they are in charge of building the experience through their actions and words. At the same time as they enter a role, students must find a sense of their own relationships to this fictional life: the *me* in the role and the *role* in me. They create alternative selves, alternative lives, and alternative worlds — in play, in storytelling, and in role-play. They discover ideas and directions that will surprise and change them. Because meanings are being made, not given, students will find responses and language powers that are unexpected.

When students are in role, they can practice language codes very different from those in their daily lives. In role, a child can speak as the leader of a village, as the one who holds the resources, as a messenger from the Queen, or, indeed, as the Queen. The context sets up language demands that will vary from situation to situation. Both emotional and cognitive commitment can provide stimuli for language exploration, freeing the students from their usual student role and allowing them to try out a range of language possibilities.

Role-Playing into Understanding: Considerations

The list with questions below points to many ways in which we can involve students in developing and demonstrating their understanding of text through role-playing. It also presents considerations on how to approach exploring texts from various perspectives.

- *Texts as role-playing resources.* What if we consider the texts we use as resources for role-playing? Which incidents from the text will students want to replay in groups? How will they begin and end? Who will they role-play? Shall we share a moment or two from their improvisations to see the unique retellings? Will we televise the work on cameras?
- *Parallel texts.* Taking a story, which incident in the plot will students use as the basis for their improvisation? They can move from the original text to a parallel story that grows out of their improvisation work. Doing so creates opportunities for comparing the two texts: the original and the created version.
- *Moments in time.* How will students capture dramatic moments in the text? Will they create a tableau, or frozen picture? Who will be in the tableau? Will there be a spoken caption? a sequence of tableaux? Will each group select

a different event to represent, so that the class can share the entire story as groups take turns observing other groups?

- *Physical representations.* How will we help our students to express and represent their interpretations through a physical mode; that is, using their bodies in movement and dance to picture what their imaginations have created? What music might they select to support their work, or will they incorporate drumming or singing as part of the movement?

- *Research for role-playing.* Finding information to strengthen and support the role-play through Internet searches for documents, books, and images will be a powerful asset in expanding and deepening the work. Who will be the researchers? Who will ask the questions? The future can open up new modes of researching, expressing, and presenting.

- *Sharing within a community.* We want our students to experience presenting their work and sharing their creations. How can we help them to prepare for their presentations to reduce tension and promote success? Will they use talking-point notes? Will they use PowerPoint visuals? Will they present to a small group first?

- *Writing in role.* What opportunities can we provide for our students to engage in authentic writing? How can the letters, diaries, and documents they compose on the theme being explored serve as artifacts within the work itself?

- *In character with technology.* As technology becomes more available in our schools, we can participate in a blog or by email as characters-in-role discussing issues with one another. What scenes will we film so we can see the varied interpretations groups have developed? In what other ways can we involve technology in our active learning sessions?

- *Interviewing.* What part could role-playing have in helping students to hone interview questions and develop spontaneous responses? Could students interview a character from the original text the group is reading? What if students develop their own interviewing situations from documents, history, or novels? Can we use technology to promote deeper involvement, as we transcribe the interviews, or incorporate still photos of the speakers as their words are heard?

Introduction to Demonstrations of Responding through Role-Play

We often see role-play occurring in early childhood classes as a normal response to stories and themes, but it has become an effective mode with students of all ages as they take on the roles of characters and of people involved in different contexts, from stories to historical incidents to invented fictions. In this section, students retell the selchie story through creative movement and tableaux, through writing in role, and in a unit built around the selchie woman's life on land and on sea. Through role-play, students begin to understand "the other" in texts and in their lives.

DRAMATIC PLAY

Justine Bruyere

Justine Bruyere teaches Kindergarten in French in Windsor, Ontario.

In the spring of 2014 I combined my lesson planning in drama and creativity to help bring a story called *Greyling*, by Jane Yolen, to life. This project involved students enrolled in Kindergarten at a French immersion school in southwestern

Ontario. *Greyling* is a Scottish tale about a selchie (a seal capable of transforming into a human) who was adopted by a lonely fisherman and his wife. Greyling lived on dry land as a human for many years until one day the fisherman's life was threatened at sea. Defenceless against a severe storm, the fisherman fearfully hung onto his sinking ship. To prevent his father from drowning, Greyling leapt from a cliff, submerged himself in the sea, and transformed into a seal. He swam to his father and gracefully towed him to shore. The story of Greyling, written for children, addresses themes of love, selflessness, and courage.

Over the course of the unit, a variety of drama teaching techniques were utilized to help students understand the story and to make an environment ripe for creativity and learning. Some of the teaching techniques I used for this project included hot seating, teacher in role, student in role, drama games, multiple endings, and writing in role. Through this article, I will explain how the drama process informed the creativity, reflection, and writing of my Kindergarten students.

OUTLINE OF THE UNIT

The "Greyling" unit of study took place over a three-week period during which students became familiar with the themes and main ideas of the story before engaging in writing activities. I organized the unit into three distinct weeks.

Week 1: The Hook	Sea centers French vocabulary games about the sea Water table with sea creatures Sea crafts Watching of seal videos Learning about seal habitats Acting as seals, drama center Learning about their life cycle
Week 2: The Meat	Making predictions about Greyling Picture walk Reading the story Posing questions/Answering questions Hearing the story in Greyling's words Painting the story Imagining parts of the story that were left out
Week 3: The Wrap-up	Creating a drama game about Greyling's life at sea Hot-seating the characters Books about Greyling's life after being a boy Wanted posters, from the perspective of Greyling's parents Newspaper reporters — "Boy Turns into Seal" headlines

Play, inquiry, and drama hold central roles in these lessons. Consequently, each lesson was motivated by the questions and comments of the students in my class.

WEEK 1: THE HOOK

From the beginning, students were highly engaged with the study of seals. Their enthusiasm was especially evident during playtime when they created seal families and used their imaginations to search for food, evade hungry sharks, and even conduct seal swimming races. Using content found on the Internet, we watched footage of seals floating on icebergs with their families and interacting with photographers.

Drawing on this information we had just learned as a class, we imagined what seals would say if those photographers could interview them. The room was "abuzz" with imagined responses. In small groups, students pondered their questions about seals and their living conditions. Some students asserted they had seen seals in the Detroit River while others disagreed and claimed that seals live only near "lots of ice."

WEEK 2: THE MEAT

To begin the second week, I organized a class activity where the book cover was made into a puzzle. Students carefully pieced together the puzzle to reveal the cover of the book. Next, students were asked to use their imaginations and predict what the book was about based on its cover.

After the puzzle activity, the entire class participated in a picture walk, where I show the illustrations to the group seated in front of me in sequence without reading the words to them. In this case, the picture walk helped the children connect prior knowledge they had learned in week 1 while making new predictions about the story based on the pictures they saw. After the picture walk, the students were read the story.

The teacher in role as Greyling

One of the most memorable activities for the students was when I went in role and dressed up as Greyling. I invited them to sit with me and told them the Greyling story from my perspective. The students asked Greyling questions, encouraged him, and even offered to help reunite him with his seal family. Many students in our classroom made connections to Greyling's life. One student, in particular, shared with Greyling, "For a long time I didn't even know where my dad was, but then he came to my house and now I get to see him." Another student supported him, stating, "and sometimes we have to live with our grandparents . . . that's okay. You'll probably get to see your mom again."

On the third day of week 2, students were curious about Greyling's transformation from boy to seal. They wondered if it was painful and what it would look like. We decided to explore Greyling's transformation, using our bodies. We chose two pieces of music: one to represent his seal life and another, his human life. When the music changed, it signaled that Greyling was transforming.

Students acted out the transformation, which ranged from painful and scary to peaceful and magical. Their differing interpretations were truly remarkable as evidenced by their comments to me after the exercise.

> "I was changing and because I'm a very strong seal it hurt me to change . . . all of my muscles are very big." (Gabe)
> "I was changing and I saw my toes change and then my legs . . . and my hair changed too. And, it didn't even hurt." (Isabelle)
> "It hurt when I became a boy because I needed legs instead of my flipper, Mme." (Bryce)
> "I had lips when I was a boy and then when I changed to a seal I had whiskers." (William)

For the next activity, I had my students play the role of a storyteller. They were to act out scenes that the author did not explain within the story. Before enacting their scenes, our class imagined what the characters might say and do, therefore increasing their abilities to respond to new information while in role. Accordingly, when the students performed their improvised scenes, they were confident and used greater verbal and dramatic expression.

Following our in-role activities, students visited the painting center. There, they illustrated pictures depicting Greyling's life before and after his human parents adopted him. Later, they presented these images with narration to the class.

WEEK 3: THE WRAP-UP

After two weeks of study, it was obvious that the students were incorporating their knowledge about Greyling and seal life into their free play: on the first day of the week, during a recess period, students created a game based on the book. Students decided that there would be sharks, a fisherman, a seal mom, and seals. As the rules developed, it was determined that a home base was necessary for the seals. The POD (a portable inflatable plastic room) was selected as the perfect home base. Next, the students decided that fish were needed for the seals to catch. Points would be obtained for every fish collected and kept during the course of the game. The mom seal was given "saving powers" to be used when one of her seals was caught. And finally, the seals would have to evade the sharks and fisherman in order to stay alive.

The next day we played Sharks, Seals, and Fisherman in class. This fantasy/drama environment removed the students from acting as themselves and granted them an opportunity to explore different points of view while role-taking, reacting, and problem-solving.

After our drama game, the class participated in a hot-seating activity. During this exercise, students were questioned by their classmates in role. The student acting as Greyling explained that he liked "being a boy more than being a seal because I can run and I have legs when I'm a boy." We discovered that he had 100 seal brothers and only one seal sister in the ocean. One soft-hearted fisherman shared his fears about Greyling going into the ocean: "I'm scared because I can't love Greyling if he's a baby seal again. I might see him on my boat but not at home." The fisherman's wife told us about her friend, Sara, who ". . . had no babies and then she adopted one and that's how she got happy. When you adopt a baby, someone gives it to you to make sure you get happy. And, you're like a normal family. And you have a crib, too. Even I can adopt a baby."

Later in the week, students were invited to the class writing center to create storybooks about Greyling's life before, during, or after his adoption. They also produced Wanted posters from the perspective of Greyling's mom.

Equally important was that the students took on the role of news reporters in a newsroom where teacher-in-role was utilized.

TEACHER-IN-ROLE INTRODUCTION

Hello, reporters. I have received word that a seal who changes into a boy has been spotted on the shore. We need everyone's help. You are my best reporters. We need to know the story of this seal, this boy or this selchie — and we need to know now! Can I count on you to write stories that will have everyone buying our newspapers?

Wanted Poster Text: Greyling

"Wanted: He has grey hair and grey eyes. He can be a boy or a seal."

"Wanted: Greyling. He can swim, he is 15 years old."

"Wanted: He's happy and if he is in the water he's a seal."

Without hesitation the Kindergarten students imagined that they were real reporters and began feverishly writing for the newspaper. Some students wrote about hungry seals breaking into homes and eating all the food in the fridge. Other students wrote about seals hiding from sharks and transforming into boys. One student wrote: "He was all alone, but he wasn't scared. He ate some fish and played on the beach. Then his mom swimmed up to the shore and got him for dinner." Another wrote: "The mom was no where, the family was no where. The seal relaxed in the water and it was a hot day. He went to the sand bank. Then his mom came back and his dad and family came back. He never, ever died. The end."

This form of dramatic writing, where the students write as a character, helped the students to add a personal dimension to their writing. Each piece of work showed me what the students had reflected on and felt was most important for people to know about.

FINAL THOUGHTS: IMAGINING, ENACTING, REFLECTING

To watch a video about this unit, follow this link: http://www.youtube.com/watch?v=bbfbwZGTOyk.

Throughout the Greyling unit of study, I noted a dynamic relationship between this Scottish tale, drama, and early learning. The children in my classroom instinctively engaged in the drama activities by taking on roles, developing untold stories, and using their bodies to interpret emotion. Their learning was enhanced by the presence of dramatic teaching methods. Through in-role problem solving and character hot-seating exercises, the students were asked to imagine what action they might take, enact those possibilities, and then reflect on their understanding of the world around them. Both the use of story and of drama helped to create a rich writing environment in our classroom. When the students engaged in reading, acting, and writing, they came to know more about the stories and themselves. In this case, for example, many of the Kindergarten students grew to understand Greyling's story from an empathetic standpoint. They engaged with Greyling's character full of hope that the selchie would be reunited with his family. Their investment in this selchie's well-being helps to illustrate the broad range of learning possibilities associated with drama and literacy.

CREATING A TABLEAU STORY

Yun Chen

Yun Chen presents a description of the response activities she developed using the strategy of tableaux. The two photos are the images created by her Grade 6 students at Secord Public School in Toronto.

What are *tableaux*, otherwise known as *still images* or *freeze frames*? Working alone, with a partner, or in small groups, students become motionless figures to represent a scene, theme, important moment(s) in a narrative, or an abstract idea. Important tableau features include character, space, gesture, facial expression, and levels. Still images can be shared by one group watching another, or the class can be an audience as the work is presented. As tableaux are interpreted, the teacher can encourage students to brainstorm the messages they think have been conveyed within a single image. In *tap and talk*, participants in a tableau are tapped on the shoulder and speak aloud a response embedded in the dramatic situation represented. I incorporated these techniques in my lesson about the selchie.

The photos shown on the next page were taken of my class during their tableaux work with the picture book *Seal Song* by Andrea Sparling. Students in groups chose a page from the text that they wanted to create a tableau for. They created their tableaux from different pages of the text. Each tableau is an interpretation of the text from a group's perspective. Students did not know what the other tableaux would look like, and they were given the opportunity to modify and use the space around other students as they needed it. We then shared the images created.

A collaborative tableau

The physical embodiment of seal

WRITING A REPORT IN ROLE

Mobeen Uddin

The response activity described here occurred in a Grade 5 class at an Islamic school in Central Ontario. The class consisted of 35 students, both boys and girls.

As part of my research study on responding through writing, I was fortunate to be able to observe the teacher and the class during the lessons concerned with the selchie story. The teacher, Ms. Amina (pseudonym), began the first lesson by generating a discussion on what fables and myths were, and the students shared background knowledge from their earlier work on Greek mythology. Ms. Amina then explained that the class would spend the next few days exploring a fable called "Greyling" involving a seal child, half-human and half-animal. Ultimately, the purpose of this short discussion was to establish that the selchie story was a piece of fictional writing based on fables and that selchies did not exist. This point was important to establish prior to the lesson so that the narrative would not conflict with students' religious beliefs.

EXPLORING THE TEXT THROUGH ORAL READING

The next day, Ms. Amina organized the class into eight groups, and each group worked with a section of the selchie story. Students were given 25 minutes to practice their reading and decide on how to present their part. Following this, the groups shared their oral readings with the class.

Although the activity went well and the students enjoyed presenting the story, it was evident from their interpretations that not all of them had gained a comprehensive understanding of the story. Thus, the next day, Ms. Amina projected it on the interactive whiteboard and led a discussion about it. Some of the students said it was sad that the child did not stay solely with the mother but was going to spend time on both land and sea.

TAKING PART IN A TOWN HALL FORUM

Ms. Amina then told the class that the students were going to take part in a mock town hall session in which they were to role-play townspeople and brainstorm strategies on dealing with the high volume of tourists visiting the town to see the selchie. Furthermore, students were asked to share any ideas on what to do with the selchie. These instructions were projected on the interactive whiteboard, and Ms. Amina answered any questions the students had, as this activity was new to them.

Ms. Amina began the town hall session, stating that a seal child, who was half-boy and half-seal, had been spotted in the water, resulting in a high volume of tourists visiting the town to catch a glimpse. She noted that this development had led to both advantages and disadvantages. She then opened up the floor to the students as townspeople. One student identified himself as a businessman selling ice cream close to the waterfront. He said he was enjoying great business due to the large number of tourists visiting the area and asserted that tourists could come in groups in certain time slots to prevent overcrowding. Other suggestions made by students included charging tourists fees and using the money to hire more security personnel and police officers to control the crowds. Some students were in favor of opening up a selchie museum to alleviate the number of people near the waterfront. There was also discussion on whether the selchie should be removed from the water and placed in a cage to attract tourists; however, most of the students disagreed with this idea, deeming that it would take away the selchie's freedom.

BUILDING ON IDEAS RAISED IN DISCUSSION

After this drama activity, students were given two days to write a short piece in the role of a town member. While some students assumed the same role from the previous activity, others decided to take on a new persona. Indeed, writing gave the students a means of building on the ideas raised during the previous day's discussion. For example, Harriot, who sold food that the selchie ate, wrote:

> We can maximize security for the selchie and his family. We can put a time limit per family to see him.

She was critical of fencing the waterfront, as she worried that it might prevent the selchie from coming on land, thus making it difficult to feed him. On the other hand, Amber, who was a security guard, wrote:

We can also ask the selchie what he is comfortable with.
Also, I think it's a good idea to make a fence which has a
voice-activated passway. The gate can only open if the
selchie or his family wishes.

We can thus see the different forms of thinking that the students presented in this creative writing task. Finally, one student, Violet, who was in role as an elementary school teacher, stated:

I think that schools should be allowed to have field trips to
visit the selchie and study it as part of the curriculum.

The writing in role went very well as the students enjoyed the activity. It also gave the students a creative means of representing and rethinking their responses to the story, having heard the ideas voiced by their classmates working in role.

DEVELOPING A SELCHIE UNIT INVOLVING ROLE-PLAY

David Booth

The development of this unit involved several student teachers and a Grade 6 class at Wilkinson Public School in Toronto.

The Grade 6 class we were working with had heard several versions of the selchie tale. During each session, we explored various aspects of the legend, and the student teachers and I began to collect data from observations both while inside the activities and while distanced from the work as observers.

The following record lists the role-play and movement strategies used in our work, the variety of activities that took place, and the assessment observations drawn from the teaching.

Strategy	Activity	Assessment
Responding to a story in role	Working with *Greyling*, by Jane Yolen, the students created the village where a seal boy lived.	Committing themselves to role Building an environment Identifying with drama context
Exploring ideas alone and unobserved	Each child, at the same time but working alone, explored the process of changing from a sea creature into a human.	Developing a character Working autonomously Accepting a role
Improvising in groups	Each group created a scene where a selchie was first seen by villagers.	Moving in and out of role Selecting and evaluating appropriately from the possibilities Taking risks

Strategy	Activity	Assessment
Taking a role in an interview	In each group, one reporter interviewed three villagers about sightings of sea people.	Taking part in small-group work Drawing on a variety of indirect experiences Engaging in the drama Revealing feelings in role
Reporting on events	Each reporter described the interview to the villagers to see if there were inaccuracies.	Reflecting on activity Making use of space Having a sense of audience Responding to ideas of others
Depicting through group tableaux	The students retold the story by creating six group tableaux that depicted the incidents.	Sharing, valuing, and responding to others Connecting ideas Staying on task
Choral speaking and chanting	The villagers created a chant to call for help in ridding the village of sea creatures.	Interpreting text Having common artistic intentions Reflecting upon emotional response
Interpreting and reading aloud	The class was divided into groups to work on sections of a story. They used the convention of Readers theatre to interpret and retell the tale.	Interpreting the words of others Collaborating/cooperating with others Supporting the contributions of others
Playmaking as a class: Sharing and appreciating a presentation	The class created a version of the story, built from their explorations in role, and shared it with students in a younger grade.	Shaping the work artistically Establishing common artistic purposes Gaining an overview of the work Employing different functions of language
Mapping and graphing in role	The students mapped out the island where the villagers lived, indicating the areas inhabited by sea creatures.	Reflecting on and reworking the drama Recognizing implications of actions Hypothesizing and brainstorming

Strategy	Activity	Assessment
Making masks and story-telling	The students created masks of the sea people to wear in the final ritual of storytelling as a village.	Understanding the art form Using various drama crafts Revealing awareness of dynamic of audience
Singing in role	The class learned the "Selchie Song" from the text and sang it.	Growing as and in an ensemble Interpreting print sensitively Maintaining mood
Exploring through sound and dance drama	The students created the sounds of the sea people to accompany a dance drama of a sea changeling being forced to leave the village against his will.	Creating a dramatic context Working as part of an ensemble Identifying with concerns of drama
Exploring with mime	The students mimed putting on and taking off seal skins each day, and hiding them from humans.	Exploring and communicating non-verbally Investigating possibilities Viewing self as part of ensemble
Doing games and exercises	The class played "The Hidden Key" (a game where blindfolded players catch another player who tries to steal a key), as a prelude to the story of the changeling.	Cooperating through play Working without teacher intervention Interacting positively with others

REFLECTION: SKINS AS SYMBOLS OF THE DRAMA

In this unit, the students also used the Role on the Wall strategy: they represented in picture form information necessary as the drama progressed. They traced each other's bodies on brown paper and then cut the tracings out. The paper figures formed skins that we first displayed, then put into a pile, rolled up, bound with elastic, and hid. Suddenly, the students' roles were distanced, but in a way, the selchie quality was heightened — these skins were symbols of the drama and of the tension at the drama's heart.

One main goal in drama is to have our students learn to reflect "in action," to alter what they are saying or doing in order to enter the work more fully or with greater authenticity. The student is both spectator and participant at the same time. We need to "hang our other selves on the wall" once in a while in order to see what is underneath our skins.

CHAPTER 10

Research and Inquiry

One of the most valuable response modes lies in the questions the students bring forward after encountering a text. These can lead to all kinds of relevant explorations and resources that expand upon the original text. In *It's Critical*, another book of mine, you can meet teachers implementing research and inquiry modes with their students.

Students' questions, challenges, and reactions to a text can lead to further research and inquiry, where the students explore and engage in authentic research in order to discover connected and enriching information, and then communicate their findings. Students need to see themselves as readers and writers when they are involved in various subject disciplines because literacy is taught not just in language arts — it is a lifelong interpreting and constructing process in every subject.

Conducting and Constructing Inquiries

In a digital environment, the new literacies that our students are developing and expanding involve thinking, exploring, connecting, and making meaning, often collaboratively. Students can take advantage of vast global networks, huge databases, immense archives, rich art collections, and interactions with experts and students internationally. Our task as educators is to help young people become capable navigators of what is often a complex and disparate landscape, "making up their own maps and minds."

We are moving towards classrooms as environments where students in the Information Age are encouraged to develop flexible and inquiring frames of mind as they sort, sift, weigh, and arrange ideas and construct new concepts in their responses to texts they meet through speech, in print, and on screen. In our complex world, where simple answers, basic problem patterns, and memorized solutions are no longer sufficient, students, like all of us, have to shift, change, learn, and relearn.

The inquiry-based classroom supports the development of a full range of literacies, as students handle the unexpected and the unfamiliar as well as the predictable and the known. In an environment filled with opportunities for reading, writing, and discussing, students can devise their own rich web of related questions that help them to respond, to organize and structure their investigations, and to develop their emerging understandings.

Techniques such as using digital projectors with PowerPoints can prompt students to consider carefully how to represent their findings. Displays and bulletin boards on screen and on walls let other students benefit from the research. The community's store of common knowledge and understanding grows as other students respond to presentations with questions, comments, and discussion, revealing their insights and feelings in a focused atmosphere.

The sense of community that teachers who are incorporating inquiry build in their classrooms fosters collaboration among students involved in working together on projects and also cooperation as community members work together as a class. Students can gain help from each other by sharing their initial questions with a partner or a small study group, breaking the topic into bite-sized chunks, helping with categories and headings, suggesting other resources, offering support with the presentation of the information — how to inform others with text and graphics or how to connect the different sections to create an overview.

- Data can be collected in notebooks or on file cards, charts, transparencies, clipboards, or sticky notes; can be captured on recorders, cameras, and video cameras; can be summarized on computer disks, photocopies, drawings, and diagrams.
- Searching the Internet and websites can provide a rich data bank for locating information; however, the material is often unreferenced and some sites are unsuitable. With guidance, the electronic search can open up worlds of knowledge to young researchers. Appropriate software, CD-ROMs, videotapes, and films can give students access to information, often in a dramatic documentary form. For example, a group of students can preview several videotapes on a monitor set up in the hallway.
- Students can conduct interviews that, when recorded and then summarized or transcribed, offer primary source data to support an inquiry. Besides in-person interviews, students can conduct conversations on the phone, by email, or on a chat line on the computer. Authors are not always available for interviews, but sometimes printed conversations are available in journals or in books about writers. It may be just as significant to interview people who experienced the incident described in a novel: a man who spent his life working in a mine may have as much to say as the author of a book about mining.
- Research sites that students might visit include another classroom, a library, a museum or science centre on a field trip, government buildings, a theatre, even a shopping mall.
- Research inquiries can lead to a variety of other print resources: magazine and newspaper articles, manuals and guides, brochures, and catalogues. Students will have real reasons for using references such as encyclopedias, dictionaries of all types, *Guinness World Records*, maps and atlases, telephone directories, or statistics to support and substantiate their investigations.
- Documents offer special insights for research: letters and diaries, wills, archival photos, vintage books, land deeds, and surveys, reproduced or downloaded from the Internet.
- Through research, students may become aware of the amazing variety of nonfiction books written on almost every topic. Using the catalogue files at the library, scanning the stacks, or conducting a Web search can enable them to locate resources that can lead to intensive and deep reading experiences.
- Fiction is also a research source when investigating an author, issue, or historical setting. Comparing picture books or novels read by group members presents a different type of data. For example, the students can map out an area of land described in a nonfiction book. They can include a key to forested areas and mark lakes, rivers, and other topographical features.
- Students can use the information they know about the topic to create a web or a chart. They can record their findings in a variety of formats, such as definitions, directories, recipes, manuals, dictionaries, explanations, alphabet books, memos, newspapers, letters, summaries, reviews, television guides, instructions, atlases, reports, articles, announcements, and journals.

Introduction to Demonstrations of Responding through Research and Inquiry

A story such as the selchie folktale can lead to all kinds of inquiries. These may be both imaginative ones and others where students add background information to their growing understanding of the context surrounding the text's origins and nature. As part of the Selchie Project, I was fortunate to be able to work with individual students on their quests to develop relevant information and to make connections to their own lives. Here, we can observe students moving into the story and then stretching outside into the connections that emerge. We can also see how Kindergarten students explored the creatures of the sea through painting and storytelling. We inquire about and search for better understanding.

THE INQUIRY PROCESS IN KINDERGARTEN

Laura Siwak with Sarah Papoff

Here, Laura Siwak, a primary teacher at Crescent Town Public School in Toronto, is working with Kindergarten students.

I read the story *The Seal Mother* by Mordicai Gerstein to the class several times to increase their familiarity with the text and its plot, characters, problem, and solution. Subsequently, I asked our students open-ended questions to generate ideas at their level: "What do you think about the story?" "Is there anything you're wondering about?"

A few Senior Kindergarten students were concerned about the seal mother having lost her seal skin. One student asked, "Why did the man take her skin?" to which another student replied, "So he could marry her and she has to stay with him." As a teacher, I recognized that this exchange revealed the students' moral development: they realized something did not feel quite right about the seal mother losing her skin. They began to question this.

Students were invited to draw a picture of "something from the story" — an intentionally open-ended task. One student chose to draw a map of Andrew's house showing all of the rooms where Andrew might have gone looking for his mother in order to return her seal skin. Other students drew a picture about the story and wrote a sentence to match their picture. A few students chose to write a question on something they were wondering about the story. For example: "How did Andrew get down the cliff?"

After our third reading of the story, I asked the students a question to encourage them to make a decision and voice an opinion: "Do you think the seal mother should live with her seal family or her human family?" I had considered handling this as a math activity by creating a simple survey with our students, but chose to keep it as an oral discussion.

Many ideas came forth from this question and showed the students' emotional involvement in the story now that they were more familiar with it. Student responses included the following:

"She should stay with her seal family because that is her home."
"The seal family is bigger — she should stay with them in the ocean."
"She should stay in the ocean with her real family."

A theme of home emerged from the student responses so together with our Arts partnering teacher (Sarah Papoff), we designed simple arts-based activities through drama, dance, and visual arts to explore the students' understanding of "home." They could do so in terms of what was special about the seal mother's ocean home, their own home, or both.

Sarah visited our class dressed in role as Andrew from the story and sought advice from the students on what to do if he feels sad and misses his mother, and how he can stay safe in the ocean when he goes to visit. Quite excitedly, the students helped Sarah to generate ideas of what Andrew would need for an underwater trip (e.g., breathing tank, goggles, diving suit) and how to stay safe in the ocean (e.g., stay away from sharks and remember to wear your breathing tank).

Students also engaged in a guided imagery activity with gentle music where they became selchie seals frolicking together in the ocean, using different body movements.

As a final activity, students worked on an oil pastel/paint resist piece of art to show what is special about their own home or the seal mother's ocean home. They could make their own connections to the story or to their own home.

Sarah Papoff's Reflection

I had the pleasure of working with a Kindergarten class over a few classes to explore the story. The teacher, Ms. Siwak, had read the story aloud to the students twice, and they had expressed clear concern about Andrew's mother being taken from her home. They felt she should have the seal skin back so she could go home.

In discussions and planning with Ms. Siwak, we decided to explore this big question: What is special about home? We started with Andrew coming in role to see the children to ask for advice — he had found the seal skin, and he wanted to see his mother's ocean home. He was upset and didn't know what to do.

The students expressed concern in this moment for Andrew and his mother. They suggested that he should go with his mother and that he could use a diving suit so that he could breathe. They also thought that Andrew could invite his father so that his father would understand his mother's world. There was detailed discussion about the sea itself and what creatures might be there: sharks, groupers, puffer fish, sea horses, selchie seals, and jellyfish. As a group we agreed that we would go to the sea next class and explore the world of the seal mother. The students were particularly concerned that Andrew meet his cousins and family from his mother's side of the family. They felt that both homes mattered.

In the second class, I used three action words — *breath*, *sink*, and *float* — and some swimming-type words as part of my narration. With my guided imagery directions where they responded silently through movement, the students improvised an underwater journey. We explored their vision of the selchie seal sea world.

In the third class, the students were invited to explore their understanding of our big question through visual art. The students drew with oil pastels their versions of home — either their homes or the underwater home that selchie seals lived in. We then did a watercolor wash over their drawings to highlight their images and we scribed their ideas on the back.

I could identify three groups in the class: students who focused on what was special about their home, students who were interested in what creatures lived in the sea, and students who wondered what made the selchie seal home special.

One student's interpretation of the underwater home of the selchie seal

INDEPENDENT RESEARCH PROJECTS

David Booth with Students

If we allow response as a class, in groups, and as individuals, students can then follow their interests, choose topics and issues that connect to their own concerns, and develop inquiry projects that can be shared and used as further texts for other students to read and then respond to. One text can spawn others.

I asked three students engaged in research projects after reading a selchie story to share their work in this book as examples of students continuing their exploration of the text through independent projects. Through their projects they explored and discovered information and ideas to enrich their understanding.

CONNECTING PERSONAL LIFE STORIES TO THE IRISH SELCHIE TALE

The first model is an account of a student's own family history, initiated by an Irish version of the selchie story. Eamonn Stewart, a Grade 8 student in Toronto, touches on three connected aspects: the great potato famine, the chance of the student's ancestor to leave Ireland and settle in Canada, and what the stories of the selchie and the student's family have in common.

Sources:
The Great Famine of 1845 —
    History Learning Site
The History Place — Irish **Potato
    Famine**
The Irish **Potato Famine**
— Digital History
Irish **Potato Famine**
(Irish history) —- Encyclopedia
    Britannica

1. THE GREAT POTATO FAMINE (AN GORTA MOR)

The potato famine or "an gorta mor" in Gaelic (the Irish language) was a seven year period of mass starvation from 1845 to 1852 in Ireland. Ireland was completely dependent on potatoes. It was their main food source so when a disease broke out that rotted the potatoes seemingly overnight, it was devastating. It even rotted the potatoes in the underground storage boxes that were designed to keep disease out. Because Ireland's main food source had been wiped out, hundreds of thousands died. Observers say they saw children crying in pain and looking like skeletons. A million people left Ireland and it is said that close to one million died while searching for food and a new life. The majority of them came to Canada or the United States. In Toronto they set up in a neighbourhood now called Cabbagetown because the Irish used to grow cabbage in their front lawns. Unfortunately even if they made it through the starvation and dangerous journey from Ireland, many died from famine fever, cholera, dysentery, scurvy and/or typhus.

2. DENIS HURLEY

The exciting story of Denis Hurley starts in Ireland near Blackwater River in Cork, Ireland, where he was born and lived peacefully until around 1840 when a great depression seized Ireland because of its huge overpopulation. Soon after in 1845 they were also seized by a disease that rotted the potatoes, Ireland's main food source. This caused a horrible array of plagues ranging from typhus to famine fever (which is basically starving to death). At this time in Upper Canada a man was commissioned to help the devastated people back in Ireland. That man was an Englishman called Peter Robinson. So Robinson set out for Ireland looking for Catholic workmen under 45 and with useful skills but no disease and brought back one boat load of hopeful men and their wives and children to Canada because Canada needed people to populate the unpopulated areas. But Denis did not make that boat. Instead he stood along with other crestfallen people and watched the ship disappear into the sunset.

But Peter Robinson felt a lot of compassion for the Irish people because he came back about a year later with nine ships and brought back over 2000 people, one of them being Denis Hurley, my great great great great great grandfather. When the ships reached Canada, Denis along with everyone else got seven acres of forested land for free! All they had to do was clear the trees and build a house. So Denis worked hard and got through a lot of trees but before he finished he met a First Nations man who told him not to cut down the maple trees. He showed Denis how to make maple syrup. After the first crop Denis sold 100 bushels of potatoes and 100 gallons of maple syrup. But he wasn't the only person to thrive in the new land. Many did well and built up the modern city of Peterborough, named after its founder Peter Robinson.

3. THE SELKIE STORY

There are several spellings used in reference to the mythical creatures discussed in this resource. Here, the student has used *selkie* instead of *selchie*, the general choice made for this book.

The selkie story links to my ancestors' story because they are both immigration stories. They both have push and pull factors. The push factor for my ancestors was the famine and the pull factor was free land and a new life in Upper Canada. In the selkie story, the push factor away from her life in the sea was the loss of her seal skin. There was also a pull factor because she grew to love her husband and human children. At the end there was the pull of her sea children that she returned to when she found her skin, but she still felt a pull to return to visit her land children.

Pictures of the models Eamonn Stewart made of the old world of Ireland and the new world of Upper Canada (now Ontario)

RESEARCHING BACKGROUND INFORMATION AS RESPONSE TO "THE SEAL'S SKIN"

The second set of project examples come from two brothers, students in different grades, who researched information on the northern seals, so that we could better understand some of the origins of legends about the seal people.

FAQS (FREQUENTLY ASKED QUESTIONS): 10 FACTS ABOUT THE HARBOUR SEAL

This summary was written by Benjamin Benevides, a 13-year-old student from North Bay, Ontario.

- Also called the "common seal" the harbour seal lives only in arctic marine coasts located in the northern Hemisphere.
- Harbour seals are generally found to be grey, tan, or brown in colour and have distinctive "V" shaped noses.
- Like us, harbour seals have different personality traits that make each seal different from another, and their unique traits combined helps the species thrive as a whole.

- Adult harbour seals are generally between 1.5 to 2 meters long and weigh anywhere from 100 kilograms to 160 kilograms.
- Adult females have a gestational period of 9-11 months which means that most females will have one or two pups once a year. This annual birthing season begins in late May and will continue as late as early October.
- The harbour seal diet consists of mainly meat but when food is scarce, they will eat plants. An average harbour seal meal consists of fish, molluscs, and sometimes squid.
- Females outlive males by 5-10 years on average just like us. While females live 30-35 years, males live only 25-30 years.
- Even though harbour seals are listed as "least concerned" on the endangered list, their global population is about 400,000 individuals their numbers are shrinking due to abandoned fishing nets trapping them and illegal hunting in some areas.
- At least, like all other marine mammals, harbour seals are protected under the MMPA (marine mammal protection act) of 1972.
- Since harbour seals are very clever animals, they are sometimes trained and featured in marine performances and perform tricks for an audience.

WHAT IS SOME INFORMATION ABOUT HARBOUR SEALS?

- Used for blubber, fur, oil and meat
- Also known as the common seal or Phoca vitulina
- Can be grey, tan or brown
- Important indicator species meaning that the health of seal populations can inform people about the health of ecosystems
- Harbour seals are carnivores (meaning they only eat meat)
- Males live 20-25 years long
- Females live 30-35 years long
- Courtship and mating of seals takes place underwater but seal pups on born on land
- Harbour seals often climb on to land to rest and avoid aquatic predators
- A harbour seal's diet mainly consists of fish, squid and shrimp
- While looking for food, a harbour seal will dive up to 91m (300 ft) deep
- A harbour seal can stay underwater for up to 25 minutes!

Sources:
www.wikipedia.com
www.nmfs.noaa.gov
www.seaworld.org
www.vanaqua.org
www.sealsitters.org
www.marinemammalcenter.org

These facts were researched by Adam Benevides, a 10-year-old student from North Bay, Ontario.

Images of real seals as can be found through Internet research

EXPLORING A THEME AND FINDING ANALOGIES: IMMIGRATION

Dianne Stevens

Here, Dianne Stevens works with a Grade 9 English class to explore the issue of forced immigration, an outgrowth of the plight of the selchie in "The Seal's Skin." The students then reveal aspects of their own immigration journeys. This classroom experience took place within the York Region District School Board.

I was excited by the prospect of engaging in classroom research with my Grade 9 English students; however, when I read "The Seal's Skin," I was dismayed by the bland flatness of the third-person objective story. Why this story? What to do with it? How to capture my students' interest?

My metaphor of teaching is that I am an almost invisible green bug on the classroom wall, my antennae constantly waving to capture the essence of the environment. I consider these questions: Who are my students? What do they need? How can I help them achieve their potential? In this instance, I recognized that the young people in front of me were mainly Asian, many of them immigrants or the children of immigrants. I recalled that, when I had found stories about Asian teenagers for our short story unit so my students could relate to the cultural background and nuances, they had responded with insightful comments. I slipped this information into my conscious brain, knowing that it would seep into my subconscious, and hoping that a creative idea would miraculously emerge.

The provocative invitation

One student, Renee, researched and discovered that Canada's immigrant population had recently surged to 6.8 million out of 35 million residents.

An idea did emerge. The young seal-woman in "The Seal's Skin" was forced to immigrate. She lived between cultures, torn from the water of her birth culture and transplanted into a new environment where she had to adapt to survive. Many of my students lived this same experience or held stories of that experience from their recent past. Based on students' responses to past literature, I believed that approaching this story from the perspective of immigration would elicit many meaningful personal thoughts.

I explained to students that the class was going to undertake a research project and that their work might be published. They thereby became research participants, not research subjects. I said I would read them a fable and we would examine it by viewing it as a metaphor about forced immigration and the struggles of one being to adapt to a new culture. Ultimately, I would ask the students to write opinion pieces about immigration. The Grade 9 curriculum at the school required that students write an opinion piece; thus, this research project became an integral part of the course work, not an "add on."

ADDRESSING BIG QUESTIONS

We began with a class discussion of big questions: Why do people immigrate? Is it by choice, by necessity, or by force? What are the challenges of changing one's cultural environment? What are the blessings? Is it important to keep one's original culture? Is it possible to do so in a new cultural environment? Can an immigrant comfortably and harmoniously keep some traditions and beliefs while adopting some new ones? We concluded that immigration has many faces and forms.

WORKING WITH THE STORY

I rehearsed the story, developing as much expression as I could for a read-aloud. I also created a short dictionary of words and terms that could prove problematic: *totem*; *tabu* (taboo); *bairns*; *patriarchy*; *feminism*; *benign*. Further, I developed five questions, hoping to give students the opportunity to extend our collective understanding of this particular narrative, while simultaneously reviewing elements of a short story. I explained that, after I read the story, students would each read over the five questions on their handout and choose the question they wanted to work on, knowing that they would present their responses to the rest of the class.

I set up five "pods" (desks arranged facing each other to maximize face-to-face talking), with each pod numbered to indicate the question to be discussed there. Students chose the question and pod they wanted. They understood that all answers would be recorded on the chart paper or lined notebook paper provided and handed in after their presentation, as their work would become data for our research project.

The Five Areas of Research

1. *The Structure of the Story*
   a) List the events in the folktale, "The Seal's Skin."
   b) Draw a graph of the plot line that you feel accurately represents the action line of the story.
   c) Label the plot graph (e.g., introduction, inciting incident).
   d) Place the events of the narrative on the graph in the appropriate location.

2. *The Oral Tradition (limit of 6 people in this group)*
   The folktale, "The Seal's Skin," would originally have been told orally, possibly around a campfire. This written version has been divided into six parts, as indicated by the hand-drawn lines.
   a) Each person in your group is to select one part and paraphrase that part by telling the story in his/her own words. Talk to each other to be sure that the whole story flows as a unit.
   b) Practice telling the story as a group, beginning with the first part and continuing to the last.
   c) Tell the story to the class, in the oral tradition.

3. *From the Impersonal to the Personal (limit of 5 people in this group)*
   There is no dialogue in the folktale, "The Seal's Skin." Create a short dialogue of 3 to 6 sentences for the following situations:
   a) The man finds the lovely, young woman.
   b) The husband and wife talk about the locked chest.

c) The mother says farewell to her land children before diving into the sea.
d) The children on land reply to their mother.
e) The man talks to the seal circling his boat.

4. *A Fresh Point of View (POV)*
The point of view in the folktale, "The Seal's Skin," is third-person objective; we do not see anyone's thoughts. Examples of third-person objective in this story are as follows: "There was once some man . . ." "Other people say . . ." "It is said that . . ."
a) How is the story affected by this POV?
b) What reasons might the author have for choosing this POV?
c) If you were the author, what POV would you use and why?
first person   third person limited   third person omniscient
d) Each person is to select three sentences from the story and rewrite them from a chosen point of view OR the group decides on one point of view and rewrites the entire story from this POV.

5. *Perspective Matters*
The perspective of the author writing this story is patriarchal.
a) What events occur in this story that could be termed "patriarchal"?
b) How would the story change if the author wrote from a feminist perspective?
c) Is the male is a "benign" patriarch?

OPINIONS ON IMMIGRATION: A COLLATION

With the interesting presentations on each question complete, I reviewed the structure of an informal essay and gave students a few basic examples of how an opinion piece might begin. Students left the class knowing that they would each write an opinion piece about immigration and hand in their work at the end of the week. The following, "Immigration: A Leap of Faith," is a collation of the thoughts students expressed in their writing, with each student's name cited as documentation for the opinions she or he contributed.

Immigration: A Leap of Faith
The Paradox

Although immigrating is a global phenomenon involving thousands (Tia), it is a huge event in the life of every single individual who undertakes to move (Shannon). Immigrating has its sorrows, challenges and blessings, as changing one's cultural environment requires adaptation (Tia). The decision to move can completely change a person's life, for better or for worse (Shannon). Thus, immigrating requires a leap of faith (Edward).

Tia reflects: "There are many sorrows attached to immigrating: leaving a place known as 'home'; saying good-bye to the beloved people there; and adjusting to new surroundings and a different culture. If I were to leave my hometown right now and move to another country where I didn't speak the language, I would feel lost and uneasy. My homesickness would be immense and intolerable. Being forced to suddenly adapt to a new environment takes great fortitude. Nevertheless, there are many benefits to immigrating; it is refreshing to experience new cultures, to indulge yourself in change, to gain a better education, and to be open-minded about new experiences."

Based on her personal experience, Alisa notes that people usually have more than one reason for choosing to immigrate because nobody wants to leave loved ones behind if they can adjust to the situation in their home country. A number of students agree that those who are fortunate to immigrate by choice are generally influenced by common factors: to be with family, better educational and job opportunities, cleaner air, a safer environment, a better system of government, better health services, improved pay, and the subsequent ability to purchase more material goods (Shannon, Alisa, Courtney, Chloe, Emma, Brittany). Shannon adds that parents may choose to settle in a new area with good schools because immigrants often place a high value on their children's education. Several stories emerged in students' writing that affirm this value.

Renee writes: "My dad and his family moved to Canada when he was only a few years younger than I am. I'm pretty sure my grandparents didn't want to leave all their family behind to come to a new country, but they didn't have the best lifestyle in Hong Kong. After some thinking, my grandparents decided to immigrate because they knew that my dad, my aunt and my uncle would get a better education in Canada, and if they worked hard enough, they would find a good job as well. So they moved; it was hard at first, but now they live a privileged life."

Angela's story of her parents also focuses on valuing education. "My father was born in Xiamen, China, but moved to Hong Kong with his parents during his childhood. My father was always a very intelligent, determined, and ambitious young man. My grandfather saw great potential in his eldest son and decided to send him to Canada for a better education. Upon arrival in this new country, my father spoke very little English and knew few people. However, he worked very hard through university and managed to succeed; as well, he made close friends with whom he still has contact. He soon met a beautiful lady who is now my mother. My mother's story is different; she was born in the countryside of Ningbo, China. At a young age, my mother knew that she didn't want to be stuck in her poor hometown for the rest of her life. This is what motivated her to do exceedingly well in school. She was determined to study hard and receive good grades in order to attend university in a big city. She graduated from a well-known Chinese university, but wished to pursue further education in Canada. She earned several diplomas and degrees from Canadian colleges and universities, just as my father did. My father and mother met through their university years, both new immigrants striving for a successful future."

The influence of family as a stimulant for immigration rang a particularly poignant note. Brittany reflects: "Years and years without seeing a family member can cause one to grieve and to realize that an image on a computer screen or a voice through a phone just isn't enough. The need to be with a loved one, just meters apart instead of miles, can make all the difference in the decision to immigrate." Tavishi's mother is an example; Tav empathizes with her mother who is sometimes sad because she misses her parents who are still in India. Tav comments: "Imagine living a life where you can't even drive to your parents' house when you need guidance. Thankfully, the technology we have today makes reconnecting easier." In a more pragmatic tone, Manuel says, "Family is a very good reason to immigrate; if you have more relatives in Canada than you have in Hong Kong, why not immigrate to Canada and visit Hong Kong from time to time?"

Kimberly and Emma refer to these factors as the "pull" of immigration, which Kimberly defines as the choice to obtain a better life in a country with a higher standard of living. She cites the examples of the Chinese workers who immigrated in the early 1900s to build the first rail line across Canada, and the Chinese who currently come to British Columbia to work in the coal mines.

Having made the decision to immigrate, a potential candidate must earn the right by passing an English language test. Tav's father managed to do this by earning seven out of ten bands (passing is a minimum of six bands), although English in India is very different from that spoken in Canada. Once in Canada, the challenge became finding work and accommodation for his family who were arriving one month later. Tav says proudly, "Moving was quite difficult, but meeting these challenges made him the man he is today."

Shannon makes an interesting observation: there has been a change in the motivation for immigration over the years. Early European travellers who lived in relatively developed countries travelled to America driven by curiosity and a search for uninhabited land on which to settle, whereas in our current society, many individuals from relatively undeveloped countries immigrate to developed countries, searching for the benefits those countries offer.

Immigration by Necessity

Shannon writes: "Moving by choice is a positive way to immigrate, but some people move due to negative events. Personally, I know that my mother immigrated to Canada from Vietnam because there was war and the area where she lived was dangerous. Usually, people immigrate to countries that are developed and provide care for them." Shannon and Renee both empathize with the many refugees who come from places such as war-torn Afghanistan and are in need of protection. Manuel adds that a location prone to frequent natural disasters can cause the same need to flee. He notes, too, that pursuing one's religion of choice may be illegal in a specific country, resulting in the "culprit" being socially isolated or even severely punished — this, also, is a stimulant to immigrate.

Brittany and Courtney talk about the reality of poverty, noting that those in Third World countries may desperately need unavailable resources and money to support their family's basic needs for survival. However, the lack of opportunity to work or the high cost of material goods may stand in their way. Similarly, for Kimberly and Emma, part of the "push" to immigrate occurs when a person's original surroundings have not provided the basic necessities of life. Kim's example is the Irish potato famine. When a virus caused a shortage of potatoes, a staple of the Irish diet, poverty and disease became widespread, and immigration evolved as a desperate way to seek survival. Courtney, Shannon, and Emma are all aware that living with the violence and vicissitudes of corrupt governments can initiate a frantic search for freedom. Kimberly insightfully says, "Every immigrant has an unparalleled life story with his or her personal reasons for seeking a better life in a better place."

Emerson tells his story of a move necessitated by his father's work. Although he immigrated to a new city within the same country, he found the move upsetting. "Hundreds of thousands of people move to new homes each year; a lot of these people will feel stress and heartbreak during the moving period, and I am no different. When my family moved from Scarborough to Edmonton to get closer to my Dad's work, it was tough on the whole family. Although my dad knew a couple of friends who worked the same job, we didn't really have anyone to help us in this strange, foreign environment. I went from knowing all the people who lived on my street to not even knowing my neighbour. It was lonely and depressing. The once familiar landscape turned into a strange new world. I felt a bit nostalgic and yearned for my parents to move back to our old apartment, but they would have none of my complaints. I was resistant and hesitant to the change.

Like many people who enter an alien world, I drowned in the sudden realization that I knew no one and nothing about the place I called 'home.' "

Shannon notes, "Some individuals and families are required to move very often and generally, the reason is not a good thing." The results can be devastating. Emma concludes: "Changing one's cultural environment can be very scary. When you live in one place for several years, seeing the same people and the same things every day and it all makes you happy, you imagine things will stay this way forever. But what if one day you have to leave for whatever reason and you come to a whole new place and you see different people and different things and you aren't happy anymore? Being overwhelmed by the changed environment and lifestyle, as well as by the difficulty of building relationships and the confusion of adapting can cause anxiety and depression."

Immigration by Force

The class discussed the fact that, in the narrative "The Seal's Skin," immigration was forced. Because the man took and hid the woman's seal skin, she could not return to the sea, her natural habitat; she had to live as a woman. In actual fact, the Vikings from Norway and Iceland often obtained their wives by kidnapping Scottish women. To this day, 68 percent of Icelanders can be genetically identified as having Scottish ancestry.

Shannon states emphatically: "The worst method of immigration by far is moving by force. Imagine being taken to a faraway land by a strange man and involuntarily being married. No one would choose this!" Courtney refers to the abduction of Africans from their villages and their forced immigration to the United States, where they worked as slaves in subhuman conditions, without the freedom to determine the course of their own lives. Shannon concludes: "If you think that this sort of abduction doesn't happen anymore, you are most definitely incorrect. In very recent times, 200 Nigerian schoolgirls were kidnapped against their will by Islamic extremists, and have not been found to this day. Even though forced immigration is illegal, it still happens over and over again."

Kimberly is aware of the plight of those denied refugee status in Canada; their forced deportation means they must immigrate again. Surely such people experience double the pain of immigration.

Challenges

Emerson opens the discussion: "No matter what the scale of the move, it will bring both curses and blessings." Jessica, Tommy, and Jasmin write extensively about overcoming the challenges of immigrating. Jessica begins by saying: "When immigrants come to new countries, they never know what to expect. They leave behind their culture, hoping for a better life in a new country. However, in the new place, the language, food, and clothes may be different. It is important to keep one's root culture but also be willing to adapt to one's new culture." Tommy reflects: "It just feels awkward for a newcomer to try the language, the food, the music and the clothes. To overcome this, you have to be strong."

Language: Referring to the ability to communicate, Jasmin comments, "Language can be two things: a bridge that connects, or a wall that blocks." Tommy acknowledges: "Living in a new community is already hard for most people. But imagine the devastation of living in a place where you can't understand anyone. You can't understand a funny joke that your classmates are making, and when your teacher asks you a question, it seems like he's talking gibberish. For most people, accent isn't really the issue. The real concern is the great barrier that blocks most newcomers from speaking to the native people. Opening your mouth is hard. Although everyone is nice, you just don't feel like speaking. Unfortunately, from my observations, most newcomers do not get involved with English speakers. If you can have a lot of friends who speak the same language as you, why would you care about English? However, all newcomers should understand that, if they can't use English comfortably, their future life in Canada will be sad; they will not be able to find a decent job without fluent English.

"The solution is simply two words: *work*; *try*. Study a lot, always have your dictionary with you, and ask people if you don't understand the words. Try to talk to people. Nobody will laugh at you or bully you. Canadians are always kind to newcomers. By trying these new things and working hard, you will notice a significant change in yourself." In a more light-hearted tone, Jessica suggests a way to overcome the language barrier: "Personally, I think that the universal language is music and dance; everyone sings and dances to songs, and people have fun."

Fashion: Jasmin reflects, "Fashion is part of your identity; a few sheets of fabric can show your mood, personality, and the type of person you are, as well as your ethnicity." Jessica adds: "You can be judged very quickly by people living around you. The way you dress is something that can either determine you are part of the society or an outcast. People judge a book by its cover. This is similar to school, where wearing name brands will get you into the "popular crowd," and wearing unstylish clothes will put you in the "mid-crowd" or make you an outcast. So, if you've just come from India and you are accustomed to wearing a sari, wear it sometimes and embrace your culture fully, but wear everyday Western clothing at other times so you are also embracing the culture you live in." Even if a person is willing to change his or her way of dressing, though, there are barriers. Jasmin says, "I found it difficult to adjust to the new fashion change, especially since prices here are more expensive than in Hong Kong."

Food: Jasmin and Jessica discuss food. Jasmin begins: "Food is everyone's best 'frenemy,' a mix between friend and enemy. Of course, different cultures have their own food and their unique way of cooking." Jessica chimes in: "In India there are samosas; in China there are spring rolls, in Canada there is maple syrup, and in Italy there is gelato. Humans like sticking to the things they know best. Let's picture this: you have just emigrated from China to Canada. For the next year you eat Chinese food, you buy from Chinese supermarkets, and you change nothing about your culture. What is the point of immigrating, if you are not willing to adapt? Try to eat Western food once a week. You are still close to your roots, but you're also adjusting to your new environment."

Education: Tommy has experienced the difference in the way Asians and Canadians approach education. "Students here are required to complete many types of projects. In Asia, the opposite is true; students must complete huge amounts of homework." He concludes: "Coming to a new country is exceedingly challenging; there are more hindrances than anyone can imagine. Even if you have great ambitions, it is impossible to achieve a lot without hard work. If you are not afraid to fit into the new culture, surely one day the sunlight will come out for you."

Blending: Katherine tells her family's story. "The most challenging aspect of immigrating is adapting to a new culture while trying to maintain your old culture. My family emigrated from China to Japan in 1992, and again from Japan to Canada in 2000. Both times they moved by choice. My parents wanted to live a better life and give my sister and me a better future. They have been through many struggles in terms of fitting into a country. What I have learned from their stories is that fitting in depends on the society, as well as the individual. In Japan, my parents were miserable because the Japanese community will not let you practice another culture. You have to become fully Japanese to live happily in

Japan. On the other hand, Canada is so multicultural that it is very easy to live happily. My parents have combined the elements they agree with from both cultures. Although it is not possible to be completely immersed in either culture, a new culture that is a combination of the aspects you agree with is possible and will ultimately bring you happiness. Immigration can really open our eyes to the world and the new life experiences that will shape who we are and how we choose to live our life."

Tav talks about the "unfortunate emotional" difficulty of immigrating as a teenager. "It can be a deplorable experience to leave your family and friends. I know this from a first-person perspective because I, myself, am an immigrant. Although I moved to Canada at the age of five, my sister was 16 when we moved and her entire life was back in India — all of her friends, her family, her plans for her life. But my dad decided to immigrate. It was a great adventure, at the time. We were the first in the family to move "across the seven seas," which is definitely something to be proud of, but when we arrived my sister realized that she really missed her old friends and she didn't feel comfortable here. It took her a really long time to adapt, which caused many problems. So immigrating can be very stressful and harsh, especially when you are a teenager. It can take a while to blend into a new culture."

Jasmin and Jessica favor the concept of blending. Jasmin says: "I find opportunities to connect to my Chinese roots by observing my mother cook or watching Chinese dramas. If I decide to stay in Canada and raise a family, I would like my children to be connected to their culture. It is always important to keep in close touch with one's roots, as your culture is your identity, but it's also necessary to adapt to one's current culture as well." Jessica concurs: "Overall, embrace your culture wherever you are, but be open-minded to the culture you live in as well."

Blessings

Emerson adapted to his move to Edmonton and now realizes the benefits. He notes: "Humans are always resistant to change. We hate it when things are out of our control and feel quite helpless when it happens. Learning how to deal with a new culture can bring quite a bit of stress at the start. However, nearly all people gain back or exceed the number of friends they had back at their old home, and the number of experiences they share with others only increases. The funny thing is that at first we detest change, but in the end, we embrace it. Had I not moved to Edmonton, I would never have learned how to skate or play GO. I got to go to North America's largest indoor mall, equipped with both an amusement and water park. I met unique people whom I came to know and love. I slowly realized that my new apartment wasn't all that bad. I began to accept it as my home."

Angela began her parents' narratives in "Immigration by Choice" [above]. The young couple married, and Angela is their first-born child. She reminisces: "Immigration has done a lot for my family. The first few years after my mom and dad arrived were tough, but they pushed through. They worked very hard to support the family while continuing to attend classes in immigration law and business administration. Finally, they became licensed immigration consultants and opened their own business; now our family is more prosperous and happy. I would like to thank the Canadian government for making immigration to Canada possible."

Mark thinks he is very lucky to have moved from Taiwan to Canada. He moved because his parents wanted to provide him with a better education and to broaden his view of the world. He says: "My immigration to Canada removed me from the Taiwanese education system, where marks represent everything.

Character? Extracurricular activities? They are less important. If I had stayed, I do not know what I would have become. I know that I would not be who I am today: an all-around athlete, a slightly-above-average student, and a person who has his own perspectives about events. If I had stayed, I might not be able to play sports as often as I like. I might be drowning in the waves of homework and my parents' expectations that I would get the best grade in the class. Removal from the system freed me from the bonds of grades and introduced me to a world of observations. I have learned how to observe an event like it has nothing to do with me, but to think about it as though it happened to my family. The experience did what my parents wanted; it has changed my life forever."

Tav is grateful for the many gifts of immigration: her parents' bravery in moving halfway around the world to provide a better education and lifestyle for their children; the gender equity that allows her to go out at night in shorts and feel safe; the opportunities that make pursuing her dream much easier. She says, "Even though I adore my culture and never forget where I come from, I am also very grateful to be Canadian."

In Conclusion

Edward concludes our class reflection on a philosophic note. He quotes John A. Shedd: "A ship in harbour is safe, but that is not what ships are built for." Edward proposes that, similarly, human beings have a natural ability to explore new territory. Through exposure and adaptation, humans thrive and change their lives. "With our current modern society making travel and exploration so easy, people have yet to realize that the true adventure of the current time is not the journey, but the adaptation to the new world."

In order to gain something, a person must give something of equivalent value, and that applies to culture. To gain a new lifestyle, a person must adapt and sacrifice some of his or her culture of origin. This equivalent exchange will help the immigrant push through and contribute to his or her success in the new environment. Important values and traditions of the original culture must be maintained while significant aspects of the adopted culture are absorbed. There is a delicate balance point that will be reached in the process of transition, a blending of the two cultures that creates a third culture with a beautiful spectrum of diversity, unique to the individual. To arrive in this enviable place, an immigrant must be willing to make a leap of faith.

CHAPTER 11

Technology and Texts

Jennifer Rowsell is an authority on modalities, and her book *Working with Multimodality* offers helpful interviews and advice for working with the digital world in our classrooms.

The Internet, e-writing, and online texts have changed how we describe and define the writing events that engage our students. Today, technology enables students to respond to and explore ideas and information in a text that, in previous times, was unavailable. The students can find background information about the content of the text, the author, the context for the writing, and the thoughts of others who have read the text, or discover connections to the text's themes or issues.

- Integrating social networking into classroom events is evidenced in new educational articles and books, alongside a variety of websites. Blogging activities (Google Blog Search, Google Reader, Flickr) are popular in many classrooms I have observed. What will these modes of written discourse mean to the students' abilities to inquire about the concerns that arise from a text they have read or seen, or to find connected texts that highlight their puzzlements or their interests?
- The techniques of cutting and pasting, inserting graphics, downloading maps, drawing and painting with a mouse, formatting, and creating books have brought opportunities for the students to respond in a variety of modes.

Introduction to Demonstrations of Responding through Technology

One major change in helping students in responding to a text is the wide-ranging use of different technologies. In this section, students from one class engage in online discussions about *Greyling* and then write fictional diary entries accompanied by personal reflections. Other students design websites or interpret the selchie story using iPads for their designs. Although you will have noticed technology being used in lessons about the other response modes, as well, here we look at the in-depth incorporation of devices as the core of the responses. Technology can change our thinking.

WEBSITES AS JUMPING-OFF POINTS FOR RESPONDING

Caleigh Dunfield

Caleigh Dunfield describes taking her first spin as a homeroom teacher of Grade 6 students in New Brunswick. Her prior experience included a whirlwind four-month resource and methods position, and a year and a half as an elementary and middle-level Arts specialist.

It goes without saying that my experience as a Grade 6 student was drastically different than that of the students in my Grade 6 class. In many ways, my students' technological literacy outweighed my own; their generation, it seems, is plugged in on arrival. This realization made my job more challenging than I had anticipated: I needed to find new ways to connect, literally and figuratively.

My solution to this quandary came in the form of an active class website. Initially, I hoped to create a simple site with the primary function being a common place to connect with my students and their parents. But when the site began to enable students to connect with each other, with peers in other grades, and eventually with an extended online community, I realized its true value as a tool to support and enrich student learning.

Our class website afforded us the opportunity to reach out into the community, whether locally or well beyond our small-town doorstep. For example, one of my students received a comment on his review of a graphic novel from someone in San Francisco; another two boys received so much positive feedback for what can best be described as their "Ode to Country Livin' " that one wrote "I LOVE POETRY!!!" in his agenda, prompting my heart to skip a beat. Shortly after the latter event, my class and I received an invitation, through the website, to participate in this book.

TEXT INVENTORIES ONLINE

We began our exploration of "The Seal's Skin" with a few simple activities aimed at having students connect to the text and consider it in a broader context. I read the story aloud to the class and then had them break off into smaller groups to read it a second time. In their groups, students wrote a "text inventory," identifying the characters, setting, themes, changes, and so forth and submitted it to me through the Comment field on our website. This allowed me to check in on their understanding without interrupting their initial interpretations or rushing to offer my own insights. Our warm-up exercises generated a lot enthusiasm in the group — no thanks to the mention of a naked lady! — which built momentum for our learning to continue.

THE SELCHIE STORY AS HAIKU

Shortly before beginning our work with "The Seal's Skin," students had been working through a poetry unit. They had thoroughly enjoyed writing haikus, so we spent a class with every student striving to summarize the folktale into 17 syllables. The results of this exercise included the following gems by Christian, Kendra, Kiernan, and Emily, respectively:

There once was a man
He lived in Myrdal, Iceland
He met one strange girl

Fat flubby seal skin
Seven babies, sea and land
Woman jumped in sea

A seal becomes a girl
She got married to a man
Soon went back to sea

Never marry the
First naked lady you see
She will swim away!

WRITING LEGENDS OR LETTERS

We followed the haiku exercise with a response assignment for which students chose either to write a legend or write a farewell letter to the fisherman in role as the seal woman. The students who chose to write legends came up with a wide variety of ideas, with titles such as "How the Sea Urchin Got Its Spikes," "The Legend of the Turtle Shell," and "From Shooting Star to Starfish." Students who opted for the letter writing seemed to take great pride in adding voice to their work, as is exemplified in the work of Gracie:

Dear Husband,

I am so very sorry that I had to leave you. I had started a family in the sea and they depend on me! I can't just leave them! They are my family too. I told my seal cubs that when I found my skin that I would return to them, and as it is, I have found my skin, and I will live up to my promises. Please oh, please babysit Lorance, Joan, Cody, Braden, and Ryleigh for me. Tell them I love them so!

I didn't think you would do this to me! You took my skin! You're a stupid jerk! Even if I had the opportunity to come home I wouldn't! I can't even think how my life would be with you forever! It would suck! You forced me to marry! You locked my skin away in a stupid dang crate and kept the key! You told me that a seal took my skin and swam off with it! And to think I thought you would never lie to me. I expected more from you!

My children depend on you! Please take care of them. I would take them with me and I would leave you behind. I shall throw jellyfish and shells at you from now until 200 597! I can't believe you did this to me! Take good . . . great care of MY children. Take care of yourself too, I guess.

Love,
The wife

MARINE LIFE: MAKING REAL CONNECTIONS

Before beginning our work with "The Seal's Skin," we took a field trip to the Huntsman Fundy Discovery Aquarium in St. Andrews, New Brunswick. Through the guidance of marine biologists and interpreters, students learned about and experienced marine life directly. They held lobsters, touched skates, examined real whale baleen, and perhaps most notably, met two harbour seals. This wonderful cross-curricular experience provided a great foundation of knowledge about our local environment and the fishing industry in the Maritime provinces. Naturally, our close proximity to the Bay of Fundy meant that a number of students had a personal connection to the industry already. Many students were keen to share family anecdotes about poor weather, biggest catches, a misplaced sculpin hiding inside a rubber boot, painfully surprising an unsuspecting fisherman — you name it!

This prior knowledge, paired with our ongoing study of "The Seal's Skin," prompted the idea to use our website to reach out to a working fisherman to discuss the line of work. We contacted fisherman and musician Mike Trask of Musquodoboit Harbour, Nova Scotia, who graciously agreed to respond to our questions between shifts on his lobster boat. Excerpts from our exchange with Mike appear below:

Do you fish with a rod or net? — Student
When I fish lobster, I fish with a wooden lobster trap! We haul up 250 wooden lobster traps from the bottom of the ocean every day. If there's a lobster we take it out, then put fresh bait on the trap and

then send it back to the bottom. When I fish herring, I fish with a big net. We catch around 20 000 pounds of herring every day that we have to shake out with our hands. It's a very messy job, and we get fish scales all over our faces!

Do you see seals when you are fishing? What do they remind you of?
— Kyla
We do see many seals! In fact there is a rock near where I grew up that's called Seal Rock. I think seals have always reminded me of puppies . . . big fat puppies! Even the grown up ones.

Have you ever seen a mermaid out there? — Trypp
Only in my dreams.

What is the scariest moment you've ever had fishing? — Ashley
Thankfully I haven't had many scary moments because I have always been careful and had very safe skippers (bosses). However, once I fell overboard, and another time I was sleeping in my bunk and a wave came over the boat that was so big, water came in my room!

Have you always liked to fish? — Jodie
I didn't like it when I was a kid, but I had to help my father because it was part of my upbringing. It wasn't until I graduated from school and tried many different jobs that I realized fishing was something I loved. All of the old fishermen say "it's in your blood," which is a saying that basically means it's a part of you, and you're drawn to it.

Do you recommend fishing as a job? — Roy
For sure! I encourage anyone who has the opportunity to go out on a commercial fishing vessel to give it a try. That includes you, girls! Some people have the silly idea that fishing is something men do, but I know many women who fish! Fishing can be very rewarding, and it can be a lot of fun. It also teaches you how to work hard, be organized, think for yourself, and how to work closely with others. It may not be for everyone, but it's a great job if you like it.

To conclude our work with "The Seal's Skin," I assigned students an independent project to be done outside the classroom. Our school put a strong focus on engaging multiple intelligences this year, and so the goal for the project was to have students respond to the folktale in a mode that demonstrated their strengths, whether visual, musical, kinesthetic, whatever.

A UNIQUE CONTEXT

Submissions ranged from comics to paintings to a mock newscast. Nate carved a wooden boat out of a piece of birch, saying that it reminded him of the kayak mentioned on the Notes & Comments page that accompanied "The Seal's Skin." Having had her interest piqued during a class discussion, Nicole researched and reported on the Canadian seal hunt. Josh and Brandon went fishing and then brought their catch to school to demonstrate the art of gutting to their classmates and thoroughly amused teacher! Students offered comments and constructive criticism to each other in person and through the website, which appeared to boost both their pride and sense of purpose.

Overall, the diversity and quality of the projects assured me that my students had successfully understood the folktale, applied their learning to create new ideas, and engaged in higher-order thinking in the process. Working with "The Seal's Skin" was a tremendous learning experience for all involved. Living in the Maritimes provided us with a unique context through which to study the folktale, and the use of our website helped us to extend our learning beyond our local area to enrich our understanding of the content.

THE GREYLING DIARIES

Michael Prezens

Michael Prezens describes working with his Grade 6 students at St. Marguerite d'Youville Elementary School in Oakville, Ontario.

When I began thinking about how I could share this project with my class, I decided that a combination of approaches might allow me to engage more students for a longer time. We had recently finished a series of activities aimed at helping students recognize and create deeper and more meaningful connections to texts, so we started our journey there. I read *Greyling* aloud and asked my students to respond to it in writing with a connection that they had made to the text and through an illustration of a scene that they had visualized while I read. The variety of detailed and thoughtful connections they produced convinced me that we were ready to approach this text from a different angle.

FROM ONLINE DISCUSSION TO IN-ROLE DIARY ENTRY

We had been experimenting with blended learning throughout the year, so moving the rest of our text exploration over to our online learning environment seemed like a natural next step. The students were already comfortable creating and responding to online discussions, and the prospect of publishing their work in an online environment, where both positive and constructive feedback was welcome, still excited them.

I began by creating a discussion called "The Greyling Diaries" and posted the text of *Greyling* by Jane Yolen online so that the students could revisit it at any time. I prompted the students to log-in to our virtual classroom, reread the story, and identify any lines from the text that spoke specifically about the emotions the characters were experiencing. We discussed these passages together and, as a class, selected the lines that we believed were the most expressive.

In our online discussion, I asked the students to choose a main character from the story and write a diary entry from the character's perspective based on a period in that character's life when he or she was likely experiencing intense emotions. Although I knew my class was fond of role-play, I was still amazed by their enthusiasm as they explored their chosen character's emotions and commented on the work of their peers in our online discussion.

The Greyling Diaries

The Assignment

Imagine that you are one of the characters from the story *Greyling*. Select one of the characters below and write a diary entry from the perspective of that character.

1. You are the fisherman's wife. Write a diary entry about how you felt on the day that the baby Greyling was brought to you. Consider this quote from the story:

    "You have your boat and your nets and your lines. But I have no baby to hold in my arms." And again, in the evening, it was the same. She would weep and wail and rock the cradle stayed empty.

2. You are the Greyling. Write a diary entry about how you felt about your parents and your home before you returned to the sea. Consider this quote from the story:

    But though he often stood by the shore or high in the town on the great grey cliffs, looking and longing and grieving his heart for what he did not really know, he never went into the sea.

3. You are the fisherman. Write a diary entry about how you felt on the day after the Greyling returned to the sea. Consider this quote from the story:

    . . . he knew how his wife had wanted a child. And in his secret heart, he wanted one, too. Yet he felt, somehow, it was wrong.

Below are several diary entries representing each of the three perspectives.

THE FISHERMAN'S WIFE

Dear diary,
This morning I had to wake up (still wanting a baby) at 6:00 A.M. to start cleaning around the hut and I was just think-ing about holding a baby in my arms while my husband was out fishing. I went into the room which was the nursery that my baby was supposed to have at about 8:00 A.M. I was finished cleaning and went back to the nursery. I was just standing there crying while rocking the baby's cradle. As soon as I looked out the window and I saw my husband shirtless so I ran outside. My husband was holding some-thing in his arms. He told me it was nothing but just a baby seal that he found so I asked if I could hold it and when I saw it, it was a baby! "Nothing! You call this nothing," I said. I showed him the baby and he said it's a selchie. I've heard of those they are seals in water and man in land but I thought it was just a tale. We shall call him Greyling, I said. I told my husband we shall never let him go in the water. "Never!" he replied. Then the day has gone by with the baby sleeping, me cleaning, and my husband with the baby then I went to bed at 12:30 P.M.

Created by Paula on June 11, 2014, 2:31 p.m.

THE FISHERMAN

Dear Diary,

I knew it was wrong to take that seal pup out of the sea and into my arms. I always am thinking about it, happy for him because he needs to be with his own, but sad that he is gone and my wife and I are alone in our hut. On that day when he saved me from that terrible life threatening storm I felt proud to be his father and sorrowful for me and my wife because I knew he would not return. When I took him I felt like The Lord had blessed my soul but I regret it because it hurt my wife deeply. But now I know he lives with his own and I hope he thrives in everything. But this experience has changed me. I am now braver to take risks and I feel like I can help people. I also love to do my job and provide more things for me and my wife. So every night I pray for Greyling and ask God to bless him. Sometimes I weep over my loss but I know he gains. And so Diary I am happy and I love my son Greyling the selchie.

Created by Davis on June 11, 2014, 2:33 p.m.

GREYLING

It was a right sunny day when my family and I went for a swim. It was my first time out of my home. I was as ready as ever! I had asked my mom and she said I could go ahead. I swam through the big blue sea, and swam until I reached a structure. I had never seen it before, I looked up to find a strange creature. It looked like one my mother had told me in an old folk story about a human . . . My mother! Where was she? I turned around only to find the big blue sea staring into my eyes. I was lost! I turned back and started to cry, next thing I knew I had been picked up and put into some sort of net. I lay on the strange structure with the strange human until we reached shore. My mom had said shore was bad and there something bad would happen to us, but she never told me what. After I realized something, my skin was shredding and I had this new coat of peach skin. A while after the human picked me up and brang me to a strange structure and inside there was another human. I liked her. She admired me and looked at me like I was hers, and I could have been.

Ten Years Later

I couldn't remember anything about the day I was born, I had asked my parents a lot and they said I was born in the house. I was pleased with their answer but I knew they left some details. I thought it was strange that I wasn't allowed to go in the sea but I couldn't swim so there was a point. But somehow I longed to, like it was calling my name. Though I listened to my parents and did my chores around the house; cleaned my father's boat and collected seashells for my mother. Everyday my father would go and come back from the sea with his net and his fish. I longed to go with him or in the sea but every time I tried my mother and my father would always say it was best to stay home. One time I secretly had tried and touched a fish. I was surprised that my hand had gone a bit grey, I was shocked! I ran to my mom and showed her, she said it was just the oil that father had put on the fish. She quickly took a towel and wiped my hand, again I was shocked that I didn't need to wash my hands to remove it but I eventually forgot about it. It had not really mattered. I grew and grew each year and never went into the sea.

Four Years Later
My years grew and the same routine went on, I had stopped asking to go to the sea because I knew there was no point anymore, though often I stood near the shore or high in the town in the great grey cliffs looking and waiting for what seemed forever. I knew this was my life and I couldn't change it so I continued it . . .

Created by Abril on June 11, 2014, 1:26 p.m.

IPAD CONSTRUCTIONS AND DESIGNS

Nadia Reich

Nadia Reich is a teacher of French to all the grades at her school, St. Marguerite Bourgeoys.

I presented the story *Greyling* by Jane Yolen to the children in all grades at my school, and they were all very interested and attentive.

The children in Grades 1 and 2 designed their own underwater kingdoms. Each group designed a different space. They considered how their environment might look and function when living under water. The children were able to explain and discuss various aspects of their spaces, and their discussions and observations were recorded with iPads.

The children in the Grade 2/3 class worked on the imagined daily life of the selchie. The program iBooks Author helped them devote different chapters to different aspects of the selchie's life, offering vocabulary as needed.

The students in Grades 4 and 5 were asked to work towards constructing a section of an underwater eco-building company. With the iPads the children were to research materials found in a selchie's environment and to construct an underwater living space based on those materials. The Aurasma app would then be used by students as prospective home buyers as they entered the model home display area. The students would direct their iPads to an image of a construction that interested them, and then the various construction materials used would appear on screen. They could read a brief description of each material and how it was used while listening to the words at the same time.

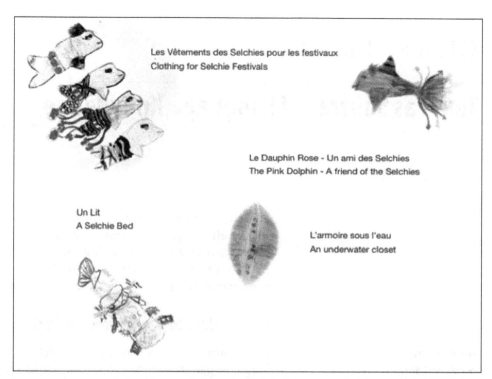

Les Vêtements des Selchies pour les festivaux
Clothing for Selchie Festivals

Le Dauphin Rose - Un ami des Selchies
The Pink Dolphin - A friend of the Selchies

Un Lit
A Selchie Bed

L'armoire sous l'eau
An underwater closet

The images and vocabulary shown relate to selchie daily living, as explored by students in Grades 2 and 3 using iBooks Author.

CHAPTER 12

Texts as Sources of Language Knowledge

Students first experience a text as a whole — its content, its emotional or informative effects, and the connections it offers. Students can then assume the roles of amateur linguists, deepening their understanding of how language works — how the text is constructed, the vocabulary, the sentence structures, the unusual expressions and phrases, the type of punctuation that assists the reader.

Responding to the "Bones" of Text

Words Matter . . .

words we hear
words we read
words we know
words we chant
words we sing
words we recognize
words we read aloud
words that make us laugh
words we take apart
words we solve
words we construct
words with patterns
words we string together
words that tell stories
words that share information
words that puzzle us
words we love
words we write
words that have families
words from our elders
and
words we are given as gifts

D.B.

Our brains classify information we meet in a text, working from the knowledge of language patterns built up from our experiences with print. We want to encourage students to use all the different strategies available for examining how printed texts work, whether they be narratives, poems, essays, or oral transcripts. Within each text, and from students' responses, we can gather the issues of language to be examined and build mini-lessons around them. When students deal with texts as sources of language knowledge, they step back from making contextual and personal responses; instead, they explore the practical details of language — a post-experience to interpreting text — responding to the pieces of language as artifacts.

Students can choose to focus on special words or phrases, dialect, jargon, etymology of words, phrases, metaphors, patterns, symbols, word play or games, puzzles, sentence structures, archaic or new words and expressions. They are responding to the "bones" of the text, investigating how language is constructed, held together, arranged carefully, and turned into meanings.

Introduction to Demonstrations of Responding as Text Archeologists

Sometimes, we as teachers have moved into the study of a text as an object to be looked at in its parts before interpreting and appreciating the text as a whole. We must help our students first to see a writer's work, a songwriter's lyric, or a filmmaker's art, and to respond as readers, listeners, or viewers. However, we don't want to dismiss how the text was developed and constructed, or ignore the elements and components that are important to its having an effect on the reader, listener, or viewer. It can be very useful for students to look at the parts to see the whole, as long as we are helping them to grow in their understanding of how the mode functions and how the language works. I call these processes that explore how texts work "Lego language": each brick is a piece of the whole, but it helps to have an image in mind as we build. Big picture first!

EXPLORING WORDS AND STRUCTURES

Joan O'Callaghan

Joan O'Callaghan is an instructor at the Ontario Institute for Studies in Education in Toronto. She has created a series of activities, based on the selchie text "One Spared to the Sea," which can move students outside the narrative and into examining the words, vocabulary, idioms, sentence structures, and language usage found in the folktale. Developing knowledge about how language works strengthens abilities to both interpret and compose similar texts.

"One Spared to the Sea" can be found at www.orkneyjar.com/folklore/selkiefolk/spared.htm. The story was collected by folklorist Walter Traill Dennison.

1. *One Spared to the Sea* is a folktale originating near Norway. Some of the words and terminology used in the tale may be unfamiliar to you. Make a list of these words and phrases; share your list with a classmate. What do you think these words and phrases mean? What makes you think so? Use a dictionary or the Internet to determine the standard meaning. Do you think that using words and phrases from the place where the tale originates adds to its effectiveness? Why or why not? Can you think of another example of a story where local dialect is used?

2. The protagonist is known only as Willie Westness. What is the effect on the reader? What does the term [protagonist] suggest?

3. Choose a section of the story that you feel is effective. What makes it effective? Concentrate on the author's word choice.
   - Rewrite the section using only modern-day language.
   - Rewrite the section as a text message to a friend.
   - Rewrite the section as a script for a play.
   Now consider these questions: How do the changes in language and format change the effect? Which do you find most effective and why? What can you conclude about language choice and the effect of form on content?

4. The diagram [below] is an inverted pyramid, the structure traditionally used by newspaper reporters when writing a news story. Write the story as a news story. Your news story should be five paragraphs long, follow the inverted pyramid structure, and have an appropriate headline. How does the news story change the meaning or effect of the story? What choices did you make in order to write the news story? How is your story the same or different from your classmates' stories?

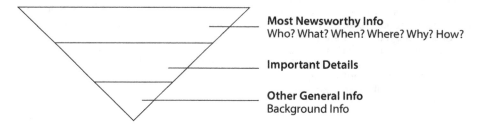

Most Newsworthy Info
Who? What? When? Where? Why? How?

Important Details

Other General Info
Background Info

5. Does the author feel sympathy for the selkie-wife? How do you know? Underline the words used by the author to elicit sympathy from the reader.

Grammar Matters by Lynne R. Dorfman and Diane Esolen Dougherty includes lessons, tips, and conversations using mentor texts to help students learn about parts of speech, idioms, usage issues, and punctuation, and how to reflect upon and transfer what they have learned to other writing tasks across the content areas.

6. Examine the following sentence from the beginning of the story:
Then it was that he heard the cry from the rocks — a moan like that of a woman in pain swelling into a loud, strange sound and dying into a sort of sob.
Break the sentence down into kernel phrases (e.g., *a loud, strange sound*). When you have finished breaking the sentence down, experiment with placing the phrases in a different order from how they are placed in the original. How does changing the word order affect the meaning or emphasis in the story? Repeat the activity with a different sentence.

7. Find a particularly descriptive paragraph in the story. Draw a picture of what you see in your mind's eye when you read it. Label the different elements in your picture so that anyone looking at it can see where your images came from. For example, if a character is smiling, indicate the word in the

paragraph that led you to see the character as smiling. How do words help to create pictures in our minds?

8. Do the Character Circles activity with [one of] the main characters. Working with a group of your classmates, draw five concentric circles and select the character you wish to focus on: in the innermost circle, write the name of your character. In the next circle, brainstorm the various *roles* the character fulfills (e.g., husband). In the third circle, list all the words that describe those roles (e.g., *loving* husband). In the fourth circle, brainstorm all the things the character *does* in the story. And in the last circle, write all the words that describe *how* the character fulfills those roles. With your teacher, discuss the grammatical terms for the different circles — proper noun, common noun, adjective, verb, adverb. Now combine your words to make sentences that describe the character. When you have made your sentences, experiment with making them longer or shorter, and changing the order. What is the effect of your different sentence creations?

STORY ARCHEOLOGY: DIGGING DEEPLY INTO STORY STRUCTURES

Erin MacDonald

Erin MacDonald is a junior-high English Language Arts specialist at Paul William Kaeser High School in Fort Smith, Northwest Territories — "land of moose, buffalo, and mosquitos rather than seal." Dene, Métis, Inuvialuit, Slavey, Tlicho, and non-Aboriginal students attend from the local elementary school and from other communities. From the building of prior knowledge to collaborative task analysis to developing reading strategies and tools, along with guided instruction and conferring, Erin supports the students into strengthening their English language skills.

Since "The Seal's Skin" was unfamiliar to the students, a whole period was devoted to using iPads to look up examples of folktales, images of selchies, and, in the case of Grade 9 students, references to misogyny, masculine entitlement, Laci Green, and a multitude of relevant current events. This background knowledge was key to successfully completing the tasks, outlined below.

GRADE 7

Task: Does the story, "The Seal's Skin," meet the criteria of a folktale? In the form of an informative poster, justify your *opinion* by highlighting the criteria (or missing criteria) with quotes and images from the text.

This poster offers six supported reasons, including some related to character, numbers, and magic, as to why "The Seal's Skin" is a folktale.

Task: Brainstorm criteria for a folktale. Based on the folktale, create a visual to represent the "pieces of the puzzles" for the criteria and example.

One student addressed folktale criteria by creating a 12-piece puzzle. Here, the top row is shown.

GRADE 9

Essential Question: What would be talk show host Laci Green's opinion about this folktale? Read the text and complete the reading tool; record your opinion in the first row on your Think, Discuss, Share tool. Use partner talk to discover New Ideas and/or Opinions, and record the key ideas. At the end, reflect on your new understanding about the text.

Below are some excerpts from the students' Think, Discuss, Share tools, along with reflective comments, where they use issues in the folktale as triggers for concerns in current events. For example, the murders committed by Elliot Rodgers had been much in the news.

1. What's important
Misogyny is a set of qualities or characteristics; a misogynist dislikes, despises, and is strongly prejudiced against women.
Elliot Rodgers, 22, went on a rampage May 23, near the University of California, Santa Barbara, and stabbed three people to death because they wouldn't sleep with him.
Why
He was lonely; he felt entitled to end his loneliness.
Men may see women as property that they should but can't own.

2. What's important
The police didn't care or worry about him [Rodgers] because they thought he was just an angry man.
Some men are extremely aggressive when denied by a woman.
Why
Our society has "normalized" this behavior and seems to accept this anger against women.

3. What's important

Misogyny kills people. Men are considered "pussies" if they don't reclaim the respect they feel they deserve and that leads to abuse of women.
Why
We need to rethink what is acceptable and make a difference.
Too much "entitlement": having the right to do something.
Marc Lépine killed 14 women at a university campus.

4. What's important

Laci Green is an American YouTube video blogger, public sex educator, and feminist. As a feminist sex educator, she has given lectures at several universities.
Why
Laci Green would think this story is about misogyny and should not be read by young children.

STUDENT REFLECTIONS

- The man stole her seal skin and forced her to stay with him. I think she would just accept it, not love or hate it. Her entitlement for freedom was not met, yet she still stayed near him.
- He thought she had left it out in the open because she was asking for it, and he felt he had the right to take it away.
- The man stole her and used her for children.
- She didn't love him after finding out that he had stolen her seal skin. She only said goodbye to her children, not him.
- I learned to have a more in-depth opinion about the folktale than what Laci Green might say.
- She didn't care about her husband because he had lied.
- Because he's a man, as an example of masculinity, he thinks he deserves a wife.
- I infer that she hated him but loved her kids and came to visit them once a year.
- She doesn't love him enough to go back, but does send him fishing luck and visits her children.

BLACKOUT POETRY

Christine Vanderwal, Shari Keast, and James Montgomery

This team of teachers from Hawthorne Village School in Milton, Ontario, chose a unique way to engage their Grade 6 students in a close reading of "The Seal's Skin." The "found poetry" distilled by the students with this strategy resulted from their attending to language and syntax in print to create affective responses.

We began our exploration of the text through a shared reading experience. We sat in a circle and discussed the story as a group. Teachers and students asked questions about what we had read and talked about language and ideas we thought were particularly important. Students then broke off into small discussion groups of about three or four. Each group was asked to think about the big ideas and themes of the story. We then met again in our large knowledge-building circle to share our thoughts. Some ideas that students had were as follows:

"Love is unconditional."
"A mother's love can always be felt."
"Every living thing has a place where it belongs, where it thrives and where it belongs."

"Animals must be treated with respect."
"Big decisions are not easy, and often cause pain."

During the next class, students worked independently to respond to the text using blackout poetry. Students each had their own copy of the text. They chose what words they wanted to keep and blacked out the rest of the text, so that their "poem" was all that remained. Some poems summarized the main parts of the story, other poems highlighted strong words the author used, and still other poems reflected the themes we had discussed after our shared reading. A number of students rearranged a few of their words to create a stronger poem.

Students enjoyed sharing their poems with others. All students had produced something that they were proud of and that had meaning for them. Their comprehension of the story was deepened after they were able to interact with the text in such a personal and creative way.

One blackout poem showing the blackouts, along with six poems copied from their sheets, follow. Some of the poems are as simple as a single representative word or line found in the story; others are longer.

1. "He took one skin
And locked it away.
A woman was weeping bitterly
Whose skin it was.
He comforted her,
But she would stare out to sea.
After many years
Wife and skin were gone.
She was the sea,
The land
and sea."

2. "The girl had changed.
Broken-hearted.
Tears from its eyes
Never back to land."

3. "Kept where it belongs"

4. "choice"

5. "One man had the key to open a heart"

6. "Locked in the woman's heart, the sea"

One student's choice of significant words

APPENDIX

Resources for Exploring the Selchie Tales

The Seal's Skin

This traditional tale represents the most common selchie story.

There was once some man from Myrdal in Eastern Iceland who went walking among the rocks by the sea one morning before anyone else was up. He came to the mouth of a cave, and inside the cave he could hear merriment and dancing, but outside it he saw a great many sealskins. He took one skin away with him, carried it home, and locked it away in a chest. Later in the day he went back to the mouth of the cave; there was a young and lovely woman sitting there, and she was stark naked and weeping bitterly. This was the seal whose skin it was that the man had taken. He gave the girl some clothes, comforted her, and took her home with him. She grew very fond of him, but did not get on so well with other people. Often she would sit alone and stare out to sea.

After some while the man married her, and they got on well together, and had several children. As for the skin, the man always kept it locked up in the chest, and kept the key on him wherever he went. But after many years, he went fishing one day and forgot it under his pillow at home. Other people say that he went to church one Christmas with the rest of his household, but that his wife was ill and stayed at home; he had forgotten to take the key out of the pocket of his everyday clothes when he changed. Be that as it may, when he came home again the chest was open, and both wife and skin were gone. She had taken the key and examined the chest, and there she had found the skin; she had been unable to resist the temptation, but had said farewell to her children, put the skin on, and flung herself into the sea.

Before the woman flung herself into the sea, it is said that she spoke these words:

> Woe is me! Ah, woe is me!
> I have seven bairns on land,
> And seven in the sea.

"The Seal's Skin" appears online at www.vikingrune.com/selkies-folktale.

It is said that the man was broken-hearted about this. Whenever he rowed out fishing afterwards, a seal would often swim round and round his boat, and it looked as if tears were running from its eyes. From that time on, he had excellent luck in his fishing, and various valuable things were washed ashore on his beach. People often noticed, too, that when the children he had had by this woman went walking along the seashore, a seal would show itself near the edge of the water and keep level with them as they walked along the shore, and would toss them jellyfish and pretty shells. But never did their mother come back to land again.

The Seal Child

David Booth

I am a man
Upon the land.
I am a seal
Inside the sea.
And when I am
Away from land,
My home is free
Inside the sea.

The mother sleeps
In her soft bed,
The child, he sleeps
Beside her head.

But when one night
A man came by,
The mother gave
A frightening cry.
She knew at once
The father's face.
He had found
Their secret place.

I am a man
Upon the land.
I am a seal
Inside the sea.
And when I am
Away from land,
My home is free
Inside the sea.

He went inside
The humble home,
And laid his pack
On the floor of stone.
He lifted out
A bag of gold,
And placed it on
The bed so cold.

One summer day,
The sun will shine.
Then I will take
This son of mine
And teach him how
To swim the foam
And share with him
This watery home.

It came to pass
One summer's day,
The mother watched
Her son at play
Along the shore,
The sea and sand,
When suddenly
Upon the land
The seal man stood
And called the child,
Who ran toward
The man who smiled.
The two of them
Turned toward the sea,
And dived into
The waters free.

I am a man
Upon the land.
I am a seal
Inside the sea.
And when I am
Away from land,
My home is free
Inside the sea.

And on the land
The mother stares,
And sheds a tear
And says her prayers.
But come the fall,
She knows the child
Will leave behind
The waters wild.
And for a time
He'll hold her hand
And make his home
Upon the land.
A sea child knows
His time is shared,
His love for both
Has been declared.

I am a boy
Upon the land.
I am a seal
Inside the sea.
Inside the sea
Inside the sea.

Note: This ballad is based on the folk song "The Great Silkie of Shule Skerry."

The Selchie's Midnight Song

Jane Yolen

The moon on my shoulder
Is no heavy burden,
The hide on my back
Is quite easy to bear,
The tumbling water
Does not halt my progress
The man's hand on mine
Is what I most fear.

The pup's mewling whimper,
The scream of the white gull,
The rattle of cowries
Washed up by the sea,
Is music that calls me
From land ward to seaward.
The cries in the cradle
Mean nothing to me.

Ballad of the White Seal Maid

Jane Yolen

The fisherman sits alone on the land,
His hands are his craft, his boat is his
    art,
The fisherman sits alone on the land,
A rock, a rock in his heart.

The selchie maid swims alone in the
    bay,
Her eyes are the seal's, her heart is the
    sea,
The selchie maid swims alone through
    the bay,
A white seal maid is she.

She comes to the shore and sheds her
    seal skin,
She dances on sand and under the
    moon,
Her hair falls in waves all down her
    white skin,
Only the seals hear the tune.

The fisherman stands and takes up
    her skin,
Staking his claim to a wife from the
    sea,
He raises his hand and holds up the
    skin,
"Now you must come home with me."

Weeping she goes and weeping she
    stays,
Her hands are her craft, her babes are
    her art,
A year and a year and a year more she
    stays,
A rock, a rock in her heart.

But what is this hid in the fisherman's
    bag?
It smells of the ocean, it feels like the
    sea,
A bony-white seal skin closed up in
    the bag,
And never a tear more sheds she.

"Good-bye to the house and good-bye
    to the shore,
Good-bye to the babes that I never
    could claim.
But never a thought to the man left on
    shore,
For selchie's my nature and name."

She puts on the skin and dives back in
    the sea,
The fisherman's cry falls on water-deaf
    ears.
She swims in her seal skin far out to
    the sea.
The fisherman drowns in his tears.

Greyling

Jane Yolen

Once on a time when wishes were aplenty, a fisherman and his wife lived by the side of the sea. All that they ate came out of the sea. Their hut was covered with the finest mosses that kept them cool in the summer and warm in the winter. And there was nothing they needed or wanted except a child.

Each morning, when the moon slipped down behind the water, and the sun rose up behind the plains, the wife would say to the fisherman, "You have your boat and your nets and your lines. But I have no baby to hold in my arms." And again, in the evening, it was the same. She would weep and wail and rock the cradle stayed empty.

Now the fisherman was also sad that they had no child. But he kept his sorrow to himself so that his wife would not know his grief and thus doubt her own. Indeed, he would leave the hut each morning with a breadth of song and return each night with a whistle on his lips. His nets were full but his heart was empty, yet he never told his wife.

One sunny day, when the beach was a tan thread spun between sea and plain, the fisherman as usual went down to his boat. But this day he found a small grey seal stranded on the sand bar, crying for its own.

The fisherman looked up the beach and down. He looked in front of him and behind. And he looked to the town on the great grey cliffs that sheered off into the sea. But there were no other seals in sight.

So he shrugged his shoulders and took off his shirt. Then he dipped it into the water and wrapped the seal pup carefully into its folds.

"You have no father and you have no mother," he said. "And I have no child. So you shall come home with me."

And the fisherman did no fishing that day but brought the seal pup, wrapped in his shirt, straight home to his wife.

When she saw him coming home early with no shirt on, the fisherman's wife ran out of the hut. Then she looked wonderingly at the bundle which he held in his arms.

"It is nothing," he said, "but a seal pup I found stranded in the shallows and longing for its own. I thought we could give it love and care until it is old enough to seek its kin."

The fisherman's wife nodded and took the bundle. Then she uncovered the wrapping and gave a loud cry. "Nothing!" she said. "You call this nothing?"

The fisherman looked. Instead of a seal lying in the folds, there was a strange child with great grey eyes and silvery grey hair, smiling up at him.

The fisherman wrung his hands. "It is a selchie," he cried. "I have heard of them. They are men upon the land and seals in the sea. I thought it was but a tale."

"Then he shall remain a man upon the land," said the fisherman's wife, clasping the child in her arms, "for I shall never let him return to the sea."

"Never," agreed the fisherman, for he knew how his wife had wanted a child. And in his secret heart, he wanted one, too. Yet he felt, somehow, it was wrong.

"We shall call him Greyling," said the fisherman's wife, "for his eyes and hair are the colour of a storm-coming sky. Greyling, though he has brought sunlight into our home."

And though they still lived by the side of the water in a hut covered with mosses that kept them warm in the winter and cool in the summer, the boy Greyling was never allowed in the sea.

He grew from a child to a lad. He grew from a lad to a young man. He gathered driftwood for his mother's hearth and searched the tide pools for shells for her mantel. He mended his father's nets and tended his father's boat. But though he often stood by the shore or high in the town on the great grey cliffs, looking and longing and grieving his heart for what he did not really know, he never went into the sea.

Then one wind-wailing morning, just fifteen years from the day that Greyling had been found, a great storm blew up suddenly in the North. It was such a storm as had never been seen before; the sky turned nearly black and even the fish had trouble swimming. The wind pushed huge waves onto the shore. The waters gobbled up the little hut on the beach. And Greyling and the fisherman's wife were forced to flee to the town high on the great grey cliffs. There they looked down at the rolling, boiling sea. Far from shore they spied the fisherman's boat, its sails flapping like the wings of a wounded gull. And clinging to the broken mast was the fisherman himself, sinking deeper with every wave.

The fisherman's wife gave a terrible cry. "Will no one save him?" she called to the people of the town who had gathered on the edge of the cliff. "Will no one save my own dear husband who is all of life to me?"

But the townsmen looked away. There was no man there who dared risk his life in that sea, even to save a drowning soul.

"Will no one at all save him?" she cried out again.

"Let the boy go," said one old man, pointing at Greyling with his stick. "He looks strong enough."

But the fisherman's wife clasped Greyling in her arms and held his ears with her hands. She did not want him to go into the sea. She was afraid he would never return.

But shaking their heads, the people of the town edged to their houses and shut their doors and locked their windows and set their backs to the ocean and their faces to the fires that glowed in every hearth.

"I will save him, Mother," cried Greyling, "or die as I try."

Before she could tell him to stop, he broke from her grasp and dived from the top of the great cliffs, down, down, down into the tumbling sea.

"He will surely sink," whispered the women as they ran from their warm fires to watch.

"He will certainly drown," called the men as they took down their spyglasses from the shelves.

They gathered on the cliffs and watched the boy dive down into the sea.

As Greyling disappeared beneath the waves, little fingers of foam tore at his clothes. They snatched his shirt, his trousers and his shoes and sent them bubbling away to the shore. And as Greyling went deeper beneath the waves, even his skin seemed to slough off till he swam, free at last, in the sleek grey coat of a great grey seal.

The selchie had returned to the sea.

But the people of the town did not see this. All they saw was the diving boy disappearing under the waves and then, farther out, a large seal swimming towards the boat that wallowed in the sea. The sleek grey seal, with no effort at all, eased the fisherman to the shore, though the waves were wild and bright with foam. And then, with a final salute, it turned its back on the land and headed joyously out to sea.

The fisherman's wife hurried down to the sand. And behind her followed the people of the town. They searched up the beach and down, but they did not find the boy.

"A brave son," said the men when they found his shirt, for they thought he was certainly drowned.

"A very brave son," said the women when they found his shoes, for they thought him lost for sure.

"Has he really gone?" asked the fisherman's wife of her husband when at last they were alone.

"Yes, quite gone," the fisherman said to her. "Gone where his heart calls, gone to the great wide sea. And though my heart grieves at his leaving, it tells me this way is best."

The fisherman's wife sighed. And then she cried. But at last she agreed that, perhaps, it was best. "For he is both man and seal," she said. "And though we cared for him for a while, now he must care for himself." And she never cried again.

So once more they lived alone by the side of the sea in a new little hut which was covered with mosses to keep them warm in the winter and cool in the summer.

Yet, once a year, a great grey seal is seen at night near the fisherman's home. And the people in town talk of it, and wonder. But seals do come to the shore and men do go to the sea; and so the town folk do not dwell upon it very long.

But it is no ordinary seal. It is Greyling himself come home — come to tell his parents tales of the lands that lie far beyond the waters, and to sing them songs of the wonders that lie far beneath the sea.

The Great Silkie of Sule Skerry

In Norwa land, there lived a maid
Baloo, my babe, this maid began
I ken na where your faither is
Nor yet the land where he dwells in

It happened on a certain day
When this fair maiden fell asleep
That in there come a grey silkie
And sat him doon at her bed feet

Saying awake, awake, my bonnie
   maid
For o how soundly thou dost sleep
I'll tell thee where his faither is
He's sitting close at thy bed feet

I pray come tell tae me your name
And tell me where your dwellin be
My name it is Gud Hein Mailler
An I earn ma living oot tae sea

I am a man upon the land
I am a Silkie in the sea
And when I'm far frae every strand
My home it is in Sule Skerry

Alas, alas, this woeful fate
This weary fate that's been laid on
   me
That a man should a come frae the
   West o Hoy
Tae the Norwa lands tae ha a bairn wi
   me

My dear I'll wed ye wi a ring
Wi a ring ma dear, I'll wed wi ye
Thou may go wed wi whom thou
   wilt
I'm sure ye'll never wed wi me

Thou will nurse ma bonnie son
For seven long years upon your knee
And at the end o seven long years
I'll come and pay the nurse's fee

She has nursed her little wee son
For seven long years upon her knee
And at the end o seven long years
He's come back wi gold and white
   money

Ma dear I'll wed ye wi a ring
Wi a ring ma dear, I'll wed wi thee
Thou may go wed wi whom thou wilt
I'm sure ye'll never wed wi me

But I'll put a gold chain roond his
   neck
A gey good gold chain it will be
That if e'er he comes tae the Norwa
   lands
You can hae a good guess it is he

An You will get a gunner good
An a gey good gunner it will be
An he'll gae oot on a May morning
An shot the son an the grey silkie

An she had got a gunner good
An a gey good gunner, I'm sure twas
   he
An he gae'd oot on a May morning
An he shot the son and the grey silkie

Alas, alas, this woeful fate
This weary fate that's been laid on me
And ance or twice she sobbed and
   sighed
An her tender heart, it brak in three

SELCHIES AS MYTH AND FOLKLORE

Dr. Bryan Wright

For generations many peoples who have lived near the sea have developed close relationships with the many sea creatures/animals, and certain cultures in the North have bonded with seals. Some of these people see striking resemblances between the eyes of a baby seal and children while others hear no distinguishable difference in the plaintive cries of baby seals and young children. The connections between humans and seals are strengthened in our interpretations of our experiences with them extending to the notion that seals are human beings under a spell.

The grace and beauty of these creatures have strengthened the bond between many families in the Scottish isles who share endearing tales of seals and often trace their family's ancestry to sealmen and thus eschew seal meat. Many of these tales trace to the motif "Marriage to seal in human form" and engage the tragic difficulty of such a joining. These marriages often begin happily, with infrequent moments of longing in the heart of the seal lover, despite the initial coercion of hiding the seal skin. However, the fantasy dissolves in the sea as the maiden dons the skin and returns, ending the union.

Many stories reveal the tales of the seal lover's care and wish for good fortune for the seafaring husband and any offspring, but other tales, such as the "Silkie of Sule Skerry," mark the return of the lover to the sea, leading to the seafarer's tragic murder of both the supernatural son and seal lover.

As Scottish balladeer Norman Kennedy relays, these traditional stories are widely popular among some Northern peoples. He retells the tale that someone from the Far North, like Greenland perhaps, was trapped in the strong Gulf Stream current and eventually washed ashore in Iceland, Scotland, or Orkney Islands, each of which these amphibious tales would anchor in cultural mythology. Indeed, the Northern seafarer would peel the layers of clothing no longer needed in the more southern climes. Still others draw connections to the pharaoh's soldiers lost in the Red Sea, believing that seals or sea people are their descendents who arrive on Midsummer Eve or the twelfth day of Christmas, shedding their hides to resume human existence.

Despite the origin of these endearing tales, unions between mortals and fairy figures have been common in literature over the millennia.

Online Selchie Resources: Song and Film

"The Great Silkie," traditional song: http://chivalry.com/cantaria/lyrics/great-silkie.html

Merlin's Cave — Seal Skin (Fable Cartoons)

"Great Selchie of Shule Skerry" lyrics, sung by Judy Collins: www.vmusic.com.au/lyrics/judy-collins/great-selchie-of-shule-skerry-lyrics-5109233.aspx

---

Index